THE PURSUIT
OF HAPPINESS

BROOKINGS FOCUS BOOKS

Brookings Focus Books feature concise, accessible, and timely assessment of pressing policy issues of interest to a broad audience. Each book includes recommendations for action on the issue discussed.

A BROOKINGS FOCUS BOOK

THE PURSUIT ᵒꜰ HAPPINESS

AN ECONOMY OF WELL-BEING

Carol Graham

BROOKINGS INSTITUTION PRESS
Washington, D.C.

Copyright © 2011
THE BROOKINGS INSTITUTION
1775 Massachusetts Avenue, N.W., Washington, D.C. 20036
www.brookings.edu

Library of Congress Cataloging-in-Publication data
Graham, Carol, 1962–
The pursuit of happiness : an economy of well-being / Carol Graham.
p.   cm. — (A Brookings focus book)
Includes bibliographical references and index.
Summary: "Focuses on the role in the policymaking process of new metrics
for measuring the effects on individual well-being of institutional, macroeconomic, and policy environments—for example, the effects of macroeconomic uncertainty and lack of access to health insurance—as well as the
effects of factors such as commuting time, divorce, job status, and obesity"
—Provided by publisher.
ISBN 978-0-8157-2127-7 (cloth : alk. paper)
1. Economics—Psychological aspects. 2. Happiness.
3. Quality of life. 4. Uncertainty. I. Title.
HB74.P8G733 2011
330.01'9—dc23   2011020418

9 8 7 6 5 4 3 2 1

Printed on acid-free paper

Typeset in Sabon

Composition by Cynthia Stock
Silver Spring, Maryland

Printed by R. R. Donnelley
Harrisonburg, Virginia

To my son Alexander,

in hopes that his nascent foray into the dismal science

turns out to be as much fun as mine has been . . .

CONTENTS

CHAPTER ONE

HAPPINESS: A NEW SCIENCE

All citizens are entitled to "life, liberty, and the pursuit of happiness."

Declaration of Independence of the
United States of America, 1776

FOR THE PAST TEN YEARS, I have been studying happiness around the world, in countries as different as Afghanistan, Chile, and the United States. It has been an amazing foray into the complexity of the human psyche on the one hand, and the simplicity of what seems to make us happy on the other. My last book on happiness, published in 2009, ended with a speculative chapter on policy, with the quote above at the top of the chapter.[1] It's either a sign of my lack of imagination or of the speed with which the current public debates have taken up the topic of happiness that I am now boldly leading off with that same quote and writing an entire book on the topic of happiness and policy. That would have been unthinkable just a decade ago.

In recent years, a number of nations—from remote Bhutan to far less remote Britain, France, China, and Brazil—have begun incorporating measures of happiness into their benchmarks of national progress.[2] Even in the United States, high-level policymakers ranging from the chairman of the Federal Reserve Board to the director of the U.S. Census Bureau have been discussing the merits and de-merits of happiness measures.[3] Not surprisingly, the study of happiness has also captured the attention of the public and is now a constant focus of the media, in the United States and abroad.

What has happened? The study of happiness has moved from the fringes of the "dismal science" and the esoteric realm of the philosopher to the center of vociferous debates among economists. The debates cover the relationship between happiness and income and the extent to which happiness metrics can be used as proxies for utility—the streamlined concept of welfare that underlies most economic models. Is Adam Smith turning over in his grave?

A skeptical view is that this is simply a temporary trend, related to the recession-related realignment of priorities, in which the pursuit of an ever-larger house has been replaced by discussions about the value of things like leisure time and socializing. Yet there are already a number of efforts under way that could result in measures of happiness becoming a part of our economic measures of progress and the subject of our policy debates. Indeed, there is an ongoing discussion among prominent academics—and increasingly among policymakers—about complementing our standard measures of gross national product with national well-being indicators, indicators that can similarly be tracked over time and compared across countries.[4]

In 2008, the Sarkozy Commission—led by a number of prominent Nobel Prize–winning economists and sponsored by Nicolas Sarkozy, the president of France—issued a worldwide call for the development of broader measures of national well-being. While national well-being indicators had been a subject of discussion in the academic community for years, the commission placed them at the center of a much more public debate. Ideological critics dismissed the findings of the commission as a couched attempt by the French to make the U.S. economy look more like their "sclerotic" model: underemphasizing economic growth and overemphasizing leisure. Yet, rather ironically, just two years later, the latest government to place serious emphasis on the measurement of happiness was the conservative government of David Cameron in Britain.

Is all of this a good idea? How can more happiness not be a good thing? And what is this new "science" of happiness all about? What do we mean, for example, when we use the term "happiness"? Do we care about happiness per se or about the pursuit of happiness? Should policymakers be in the business of telling people what will make them happy?[5] And whose happiness do we care about? Do we care about the happiness of isolated individuals? The happiness of nations? Or about happiness in some broader global sense?

In the end, the new and rich debates on happiness and policy, on national well-being indicators, and on measures of gross national happiness, among others, are raising the same fundamental question. How can studies of happiness help us to better evaluate the state of human welfare and well-being, in both the present and the future? The tools introduced by happiness economics provide us with broader measures of well-being than do income data alone, and they allow us to test and attach relative weights to the effects of all sorts of conditions, ranging from environmental degradation and commuting time to crime and unemployment rates to smoking and exercising. They are new and powerful tools for scholars and, perhaps, for policymakers.

Yet introducing broader measures of well-being into the policy arena also raises a host of unanswered questions. Among them is a conundrum raised repeatedly by my research: the paradox of happy peasants and frustrated achievers. While poor people are less happy than wealthy people *on average* in countries around the world, very poor people often report that they are very happy. In fact, they often report higher levels of happiness than their slightly wealthier counterparts and at times even higher levels than the very rich (miserable millionaires). This puzzle is explained in part by people's ability to adapt to adversity and related differences in norms and expectations. While better accounting for differences in norms, expectations, and capacity to adapt can enhance our understanding of human well-being, they also complicate comparisons based on well-being data.

My primary objective in this book is to discuss the promise—and potential pitfalls—of delving into the policy realm with happiness research and indicators. In the next chapter, I review the different definitions and conceptions of happiness and provide some examples of how those definitions—such as happiness defined as contentment in the Benthamite sense, or as the opportunity to lead a fulfilling life in the Artistotelian sense—help explain some key relationships, such as that between happiness and income. The definition of happiness also seems to vary across people and societies and thereby helps to explain the paradox of happy peasants and frustrated achievers.

In particular, I focus on the question of whether policy should be concerned with happiness *per se*—for example, happiness with day-to-day life—or with the opportunity to pursue happiness in the sense of building a fulfilling life, as the quote from the Declaration of Independence at the top of this chapter suggests. In other words, should we be listening to Bentham or to Aristotle as we think about happiness in the policy realm? On what basis—theoretical, empirical, or normative—should we make that decision?

In chapter 3, I review what we know about happiness in the United States and around the world, based on my own research and that of several other scholars (that chapter can be skipped by those readers already familiar with the literature). In chapter 4, I focus on the unanswered questions that are posed by the empirical research and, in particular, the conundrum posed by people's ability to adapt to a wide range of phenomena, including crime, corruption, poverty, and poor health, and still report being happy.

In chapter 5, I attempt to bring these issues to bear on the policy debate, both in terms of what they imply for our concrete attempts to develop operational measures of well-being and in terms of deeper philosophical questions about which dimensions of human welfare public policy should be most concerned about. Accepting that determining which dimensions of human welfare are most important to policy poses difficulties for both method and economic theory, I believe that the effort to do so will force us to think deeply and productively about what measures of human well-being are the most accurate benchmarks of economic progress and human development.

A NOTE ON TERMINOLOGY

Before we delve into the deeper conceptual questions or even a description of the general approach taken here, it is important to clarify what we mean when we use the terms "happiness," "well-being," "subjective well-being," and "life satisfaction," among others. They are often used interchangeably in the economics literature, while psychologists take much more care in distinguishing the nuances between them. Meanwhile, the nascent discussion on policy, described in detail throughout the book, is forcing more definitional clarity precisely because the differences in the meaning of these terms could have vastly different policy implications.

While the terms are related, they have distinct meanings. "Happiness" is perhaps the most open-ended and least well-defined of the terms, although it is the one that gets the most public attention and interest. It is also the term that appears in the U.S. Declaration of Independence. A happiness question attempts to gauge how happy people feel about their lives in general. As discussed below, from an empirical research perspective, this question is useful precisely because it does not impose a definition of happiness on the respondents and they conceptualize happiness for themselves.

"Life satisfaction" is a closely related term, and responses to questions about life satisfaction correlate very closely with those to happiness questions. Yet it is slightly more narrowly framed than the term "happiness," and it correlates a bit more closely with income. It is likely that when people are asked about their satisfaction with their lives, as opposed to happiness in general, they are more likely to evaluate their life circumstances as a whole in addition to their happiness at the moment.

The ladder-of-life question, introduced by sociologist Howard Cantril decades ago and now an integral part of the Gallup World Poll, is also often used interchangeably with the question of happiness as a research tool. However, it is a more framed question in that it introduces a relative component by asking respondents to compare their lives to the best possible life that they can imagine. Not surprisingly, responses to the ladder-of-life question correlate even more closely with income than do either happiness or life satisfaction questions, as most respondents compare their lives to a national or international reference norm.

"Subjective well-being" is a term that encompasses all of the ways in which people report their well-being, from open-ended happiness to satisfaction with different domains, such as work, health, and education, among others. Psychologists in particular conduct separate analyses of each of these domains, comparing the results of each with particular variables of interest. As is discussed throughout the book, the definition on which the analysis is based can result in quite different conclusions, with varying degrees of relevance for policy. "Well-being," finally, is the most encompassing of all of the terms: it implies an evaluation of human welfare that extends beyond the components that income can accurately capture or measure.

THE ECONOMICS OF HAPPINESS: AN INTRODUCTION TO THE APPROACH

The study of happiness, long the purview of psychologists, is a fairly new venture in economics. Indeed, the research was initially eschewed by the economics profession. Yet there are now literally thousands of articles based on happiness surveys in mainstream journals; panels on happiness abound at economics association meetings; and happiness research was even featured at the 2011 World Economics Forum in Davos, the annual pinnacle of networking for bankers, business people, and finance ministers.

The economics of happiness approach provides us with new tools and data with which to develop measures of welfare that include income metrics but also extend well beyond those metrics. This approach does not purport to replace income-based measures of welfare but instead to complement them with broader measures of well-being. Those measures are based on the results of large-scale surveys, across countries and over time, of hundreds of thousands of individuals who are asked to assess their own welfare. The surveys provide information about the importance of a range of factors that affect well-being; they include income but also highlight others, such as health, marital and employment status, and civic trust.

The new metrics allow us to place relative weights on the cost of things like a lost job, a divorce, various health conditions, commuting time, and even uncertainty. On the other hand, they also allow us to evaluate the benefits of participating in democracy, of being part of a civic organization, and of exercising, among other things.

This approach departs from economists' standard reliance on revealed preferences as measures of welfare. Put more simply, traditional economic analysis is based on the assumption that information in survey data cannot be believed. Because there are no consequences to what people say, the only credible data come from revealed consumption choices, made within a fixed budget constraint and entailing genuine trade-offs.

Because we cannot look into a man's soul and find out how happy he really is, traditional microeconomics argues that it is best to judge his happiness from measures based on how he behaves. . . . The empirical analysis of revealed preferences has produced a number of fairly robust results. Amongst these are that people regularly act as if they prefer to have more than less money. Most people want bigger rather than smaller houses. . . . The money metric of utility is an offspring of the revealed preferences approach. . . . We can therefore measure the revealed preference utility associated with a good using the price that an individual is willing to pay for it.[6]

Happiness economics departs from that assumption and uses data derived from surveys—for example, data based on expressed preferences rather than revealed choices. That departure has support from a large body of research in behavioral economics, which has gone a long way in showing how "homo sapiens" departs from the hyper-rational, calculating "homo economicus" that underlies most traditional economic models.[7] Behavioral economics research shows that many choices that consumers—and people in general—make are not rational, preference-maximizing choices. Some reflect loss aversion: individuals tend to value something that they already own much more than can be measured by the amount that they were willing to pay for it in the first place.

The example highlighted in well-known work by Daniel Kahneman—in which individuals would not pay more than $2 for a coffee mug, but once they owned it, refused to sell it for less than $4—comes to mind.[8] Other choices may be driven by norms, addiction, or self-control problems rather than by rational choice. Revealed preferences assess the consumption behavior of the obese or of smokers as the result of rational, welfare-enhancing choices, for example, while the detrimental effects of those choices are immediately obvious to the outside (non-economist?) observer.

Happiness economics, therefore, is especially well-suited to answering questions in areas where revealed preferences provide limited information. For example, revealed preferences cannot fully gauge the welfare effects of particular policies or institutional arrangements that individuals are powerless to change and with respect to which they therefore cannot make a choice or take an action that reveals a preference. Examples include the welfare effects of inequality, environmental degradation, and macroeconomic factors such as inflation and unemployment. Along the same lines, the approach is also especially well-suited to evaluating the relative weights that people place on different public goods. The latter are, by definition, difficult to value by taking the consumption-based revealed preferences approach. Yet happiness or life satisfaction surveys can be used to measure the value that people attribute to, for example, clean air and safe neighborhoods, even though they do not make consumption choices as a means of expressing their preferences (at least short of picking up and moving to a different location, which is a rather daunting choice for many people).

Imagine, for example, a poor peasant in Bolivia who is made very unhappy by inequality or by poor governance. Short of emigrating or protesting, it is difficult to imagine how he or she can reveal a preference. Yet those institutional arrangements may have major welfare consequences that can be observed only through expressed preferences, as captured by survey data. In many of his writings, Amartya Sen criticizes economists' excessive focus on choice as a sole indicator of human behavior. His capabilities-based approach to poverty highlights the lack of capacity of the poor to make certain choices or to take certain actions.[9] Well-being surveys give us a metric with which we can assess the welfare effects of situations in which choice is constrained or absent altogether.

Another area in which the revealed preferences approach is limited and happiness surveys can shed light is the welfare effects of addictive behaviors such as smoking and drug abuse and of obesity. While standard approaches assess the consumption behavior of the obese or of smokers as the result of welfare-enhancing choices, research based on happiness surveys (both mine with Andy Felton and that of some others) finds that obese individuals are much less happy than average and that cigarette taxes make smokers happier.[10] Those results make sense only if obesity and smoking are considered the result of problems with addiction and self-control rather than the result of optimal revealed preferences.

Happiness surveys are based on questions in which the individual is asked, for example, "Generally speaking, how happy are you with your life?" or "How satisfied are you with your life?" Possible answers are ranked on a scale of from 4 to 10 points. As noted above, answers to happiness and life satisfaction questions correlate quite closely, and economists use them interchangeably.[11] Psychologists, meanwhile, typically use a wider range of questions, from those that measure emotional states (affect), such as whether the respondent was feeling worried or smiled frequently the day before, to those that seek to evaluate life as a whole in a broader sense, such as life purpose or life satisfaction questions. Ongoing research by both psychologists and economists is exploring the relationship of different questions and variables of interest, such as income, and exploring which are the most suitable for use in measures relevant to policy.

The happiness-based approach is not without methodological challenges.[12] My own research suggests that the deepest challenge is assessing the extent to which answers to the surveys are biased by the context in which individuals live and the capabilities or agency that they have. For example, how comparable are the answers of a destitute peasant who reports being very happy, either because he has low expectations or because he has a naturally cheerful disposition (or both), and those of a very wealthy individual in a developed economy who reports being miserable, either because he holds raised expectations related to affluence and opportunity that are held by members of his society in general or because he is a natural curmudgeon (or both)?

Some critics—Sen included—believe that the answer of the happy peasant is merely misinformed by lack of information and agency and therefore is of no consequence. That conclusion suggests that it is in the purview of policymakers to tell people what will make them better off, or more simply put, happier. My own view, in contrast, is that there is a great deal that can be learned through deeper understanding of what underlies people's responses to such survey questions, even though there are measurement and comparability problems that must be addressed.

A related challenge is determining the extent to which people either are bad judges of what makes them happy or mis-predict what will make them happy in the future, or both.[13] The result in some instances is perverse consumption and other behavioral choices that can be detrimental to the welfare of the individuals making them. While that is indeed an issue, it is not one that is unique to happiness surveys in gauging individual welfare. Income- or consumption-based measures consider all forms of consumption as positive in the utility function (albeit with decreasing marginal returns) even if consumption actually undermines well-being, as in the case of nicotine-addicted individuals smoking cigarettes or of morbidly obese individuals eating junk food.

The very consistent patterns that we find in the standard correlates of happiness across very large samples of individuals across countries and over time suggest that these correlates—which include income but also measures of health, friendship, and access to opportunities and purposeful employment, among other things—may be more consistent measures of human well-being than are consumption choices, which vary more—both across individuals and in their welfare effects—once very basic needs are met. Therefore the extent to which individuals mis-predict what will make them happy remains a challenge for income-based as well as survey-based measures of welfare.

Other methodological problems are solved more simply. Happiness questions must be placed at the beginning of surveys, so they are not framed or biased by prior questions, such as those about the sufficiency of the respondent's income or the state of his or her marriage.[14] As with all economic measurements, the answer of any specific individual may be biased by idiosyncratic, unobserved events. Bias in answers to happiness surveys can also result from unobserved personality traits and correlated measurement errors (which can be corrected by econometric techniques that correct for individual personality traits if and when data for the same respondents are available over time—for example, panel data.[15]

Most of the biases and potential errors in the happiness data are common to all survey data. Indeed, respondents probably have *less* incentive to be dishonest in responding to questions about their happiness than they do in responding to questions about their income. While answers to questions about happiness can surely be biased by strong cultural norms (for example, if it is a point of national pride to be positive), underreporting of income is a problem that afflicts income surveys in countries at all levels of development.

Despite all of the potential problems, cross-sections of large samples across countries and over time find remarkably consistent patterns in the determinants of happiness.[16] In addition, psychologists find validation in the way that people answer happiness surveys based on physiological measures of happiness, such as frontal activity in the brain and the number of "genuine"—Duchenne—smiles.[17]

While it is impossible to measure the precise effects of these variables on each individual's actual happiness, we can use the coefficients in happiness equations to assign relative weights to them for the average person. Danny Blanchflower and Andrew Oswald pioneered this approach over a decade ago, based on data from the United States and Britain, in estimating how much income a typical individual in the United States or Britain would need to experience a level of happiness sufficient to compensate for the loss in well-being resulting from, for example, divorce ($100,000 would be required) or job loss ($60,000 would be required).[18]

Given the methodological and philosophical questions raised above, those figures should be interpreted as relative orders of magnitude rather than as precise income measures. Happiness equations explain only a small amount of the variance in reported happiness; much is driven by innate character traits, by genes, and by other unobservable variables.[19] As a result, scholars are increasingly delving into the realms of genetics, psychology, and other disciplines to disentangle the relative importance of these various phenomena, and despite the challenges entailed in doing so—or perhaps because of them—they are generating novel and exciting areas of research.

WHAT WE CAN LEARN FROM HAPPINESS SURVEYS

What is most remarkable is how stable the standard determinants of happiness are in countries worldwide, regardless of their level of development. Everywhere that I have studied happiness some very simple patterns hold: a stable marriage, good health, and enough (but not too much) income are good for happiness. Unemployment, divorce, and economic instability are terrible for happiness—everywhere that happiness is studied. Age and happiness have a remarkably consistent U-shaped relationship, with the turning point in the mid- to late forties, at which point happiness increases with age as long as health and partnerships stay sound. Among other things, this relationship reflects an alignment of expectations and reality as people "grow up." Indeed, I have studied this relationship in countries as diverse as Uzbekistan, Great Britain, Chile, and Afghanistan, and it holds in all of them, with modest differences in the turning point (see chapter 3 for a detailed discussion).

The stability in the standard determinants of happiness allows us to control for those determinants in large samples of respondents and to look at the differential effects of other variables of interest across individuals, socioeconomic cohorts, or countries. Other variables can range from the welfare effects of institutional arrangements such as inequality or governance structures to the effects of environmental quality or commuting time to the effects of behaviors such as exercising, drinking, or smoking.

Some studies have attempted to separate the effects of income from those of other related factors, such as satisfaction in the workplace. Studies of unexpected lottery gains find that these isolated gains have positive effects on happiness, although it is not clear that they are of a lasting nature.[20] Other studies have explored causality from the reverse direction and found that people with higher levels of happiness tend to perform better in the labor market and to earn more income in the future.[21]

A question that constantly raises debate among economists—and politicians—is how income inequality affects individual welfare. Happiness surveys provide new insights. The results seem to depend on the context. Most studies of the United States and Europe find that inequality has modest or insignificant effects on happiness. Indeed, rather remarkably, the people in the United States who are made unhappy by inequality are left-leaning rich people![22] In contrast, my research on Latin America with Andy Felton finds that inequality is negative for the well-being of the poor and positive for the rich.[23]

The mixed results reflect the fact that inequality can be a signal of future opportunity and mobility as much as it can be a sign of injustice, and in the United States the opportunity interpretation still predominates. Objective data, however, do not show U.S. mobility rates to be higher than average for countries that are members of the Organization for Economic Cooperation and Development (OECD). In Latin America, where inequality is much greater and where public institutions and labor markets are notoriously inefficient, inequality signals persistent disadvantage or advantage rather than opportunity and mobility (even though mobility rates in some countries are at least as high as in the United States).[24]

Happiness surveys also facilitate the measurement of the effects of broader, non-income components of inequality, such as race, gender, and status, all of which are found to be highly significant.[25] That finding is supported by work in the health arena, which finds that relative social standing has significant effects on health outcomes.[26] Happiness research can also deepen our understanding of poverty. For example, while the happy peasant and miserable millionaire conundrum contradicts the standard finding that poor people are less happy than wealthier people within countries, it suggests the role that low expectations play in explaining persistent poverty in some cases.

Happiness surveys can be used to examine the effects of different macro-policy arrangements on well-being. Most studies find that inflation and unemployment have negative effects on happiness. The effects of unemployment are stronger than those of inflation and hold above and beyond the effects of forgone income.[27] The standard "misery index," which assigns equal weight to inflation and unemployment, may be underestimating the effects of the latter on well-being.[28]

Happiness research also shows that political arrangements matter. Much of the literature finds that both trust and freedom have positive effects on happiness.[29] Research based on variance in voting rights across cantons in Switzerland finds that there are positive effects from *participating* in direct democracy.[30] My research in Latin America finds a strong positive correlation between happiness and preference for democracy.[31]

Happiness surveys can also help gauge the welfare effects of various public policies. How does a tax on addictive substances, such as tobacco and alcohol, for example, affect well-being? The above-cited study on cigarette taxes suggests that the negative financial effects may be outweighed by positive self-control effects. How would placing a tax on junk food (one among many factors related to obesity) affect the happiness of the obese? My research with Andy Felton suggests that the consumption choices of the obese are not necessarily making them happy; perhaps a junk food tax would be less deleterious than an income-based evaluation would predict.

In short, it seems that the world is our oyster and happiness surveys can help us develop a much broader understanding of human well-being—and its determinants—than income data alone can. It all seems rather logical and simple and suggests rather straightforward policy recommendations, such as placing emphasis on health, jobs, and economic stability as much as on economic growth. Bring on National Well-Being Indicators!

Yet precisely because human well-being is a more complex state than income data alone can measure—because it is determined by some combination of exogenous factors related to the environment and endogenous traits related to individuals' genetic and psychological make-up, among other things—there are also some as yet unresolved conundrums that pose challenges for the foray into the policy arena. Foremost among them, in my view, is the remarkable human capacity to adapt to both prosperity and adversity. The discussion of the Easterlin paradox that follows here touches on this topic. Some of the results from my recent studies of happiness around the world bring this conundrum front and center.

THE BIG DEBATE: HOW MUCH INCOME MATTERS TO HAPPINESS

In his original study in the mid-1970s, Richard Easterlin—the first modern economist to study happiness—revealed a paradox that sparked interest in the topic but is still unresolved. While most happiness studies find that *within* countries wealthier people are, on average, happier than poor ones, studies across countries and over time find very little, if any, relationship between increases in per capita income and average happiness levels. On average,

FIGURE 1-1. Life Satisfaction and GDP per Capita, Select Countries, 1998–2008[a]

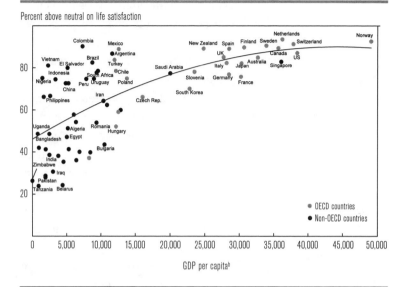

Source: Author's calculations with Soumya Chattopadhyay (March 2011) using World Values Survey (for life satisfaction) and World Bank *World Development Indicators* (for GDP per capita).
a. R-squared equals 0.498.
b. Purchasing power parity, constant 2005 international dollars.

wealthier countries (as a group) are happier than poor ones (as a group); happiness seems to rise with income up to a certain point, but not beyond it. Yet even among the less happy, poorer countries, there is not a clear relationship between average income and average happiness level, suggesting that many other factors—including cultural traits—are at play (see figure 1-1).

Within countries, income matters to happiness.[32] Deprivation and abject poverty in particular are very bad for happiness. Yet after basic needs are met, factors other than income—such as rising aspirations, relative income differences, and the security of gains—become increasingly important. Long before the economics of happiness was established, James Duesenberry (1949) noted the impact of changing aspirations on income satisfaction and its potential effects on consumption and saving rates. Any number of happiness studies have since confirmed the effects of rising aspirations and also have noted their potential role in driving excessive consumption and other perverse economic behaviors.[33]

Therefore, a common interpretation of the Easterlin paradox is that humans are on a "hedonic treadmill": aspirations increase along with income and, after basic needs are met, relative rather than absolute levels of income matter to well-being. Another interpretation of the paradox is the psychologists' "set point" theory of happiness, in which every individual is presumed to have a happiness level that he or she goes back to over time, even after major changes in that level brought on by events such as winning the lottery or getting divorced.[34] The implication of that interpretation for policy is that nothing much can be done to increase happiness.

Individuals are remarkably adaptable, and in the end they can get used to most things, income gains in particular. The behavioral economics literature, for example, shows that individuals value losses more than gains, as in the case of the coffee mug example cited above.[35] In addition, Easterlin argues that individuals adapt more in the pecuniary arena than in the non-pecuniary arena, while life-changing events such as bereavement have lasting effects on happiness. DiTella and MacCulloch find that the happiness effects associated with a raise in salary last barely one year, while those associated with a promotion last at least five years.[36] Yet because most policy is based on income-based measures of well-being, it overemphasizes the importance of income gains to well-being and underestimates that of other factors, such as health, family, and stable employment.

There is no consensus about which interpretation is more accurate. In recent years there has been a renewed debate about whether or not the Easterlin paradox holds. A recent study by Betsey Stevenson and Justin Wolfers and another by Angus

Deaton, based on new data from the Gallup World Poll, find a consistent log-linear, cross-country relationship between income and happiness, directly challenging Easterlin's findings.[37] That finding has resulted in a heated and at times even acrimonious debate among economists.

Rather ironically, both sides of the debate may be correct. One reason is substantive: on the one hand, it makes sense that people in richer countries are happier than those in destitute countries and on the other, many things other than income contribute to people's happiness, regardless of their level of income. Many of those things—like freedom, stable employment, and good health—are easier to come by in wealthier countries. Still, there is plenty of variance in their availability, even across countries with comparable income levels.

The other reason is methodological. The later studies use new data from the Gallup World Poll, which include many more observations from small poor countries in Africa and from the transition economies than did Easterlin's original data. The transition countries in particular have relatively low levels of happiness, in part because happiness levels fell markedly with the painful structural changes that accompanied the collapse of centrally planned economies. And some of the sub-Saharan African countries have had flat or even negative rates of growth over time. Therefore the story may be one of falling or volatile income trajectories pulling down happiness at the bottom rather than one of higher levels of income pulling up happiness at the top. There is, however, a wide debate over the extent to which that is the case.

There is more agreement on the influence of different questions on the results. Easterlin's work is based on surveys that used open-ended happiness or life satisfaction questions ("Generally speaking, how happy are you with your life?" "Generally speaking, how satisfied are you with your life?"), with possible answers ranging from "Not at all" to "Very" on a 4- or 5-point scale. The

Gallup World Poll uses Cantril's "ladder of life"question: "Please imagine a ladder with steps from zero at the bottom to ten at the top. The top of the ladder represents the best possible life for you and the bottom of the ladder represents the worst possible life for you. On which step would you say you personally feel you stand at this time?"

Both sets of questions are reasonable gauges of happiness, broadly defined, and both correlate in a similar manner with the usual variables. Research based on all of the questions finds that, on average, stable marriage, good health, and enough income are good for happiness (although how much income is enough varies across countries) and that unemployment, divorce, and economic instability are bad for happiness.

At the same time, there is some variance in the findings based on different questions. As noted above, the best-possible-life/ ladder-of-life question is more framed than the open-ended happiness questions, asking respondents to make a relative comparison when they assess their lives. Mario Picon, Soumya Chattopadhyay, and I compared how the various questions correlated with key variables of interest in the Gallup World Poll for Latin America. We found that the answers to the best-possible-life question correlated more closely with income—both across and within countries—than open-ended happiness questions and that the difference was greater across countries than within them.[38]

Our results from Afghanistan underscore the same point. Afghanis scored higher than the world average on an open-ended happiness question, on par with respondents in Latin America, where material conditions, viewed objectively, are much better. Afghanis were also 20 percent more likely to smile in a day than were Cubans. Yet when asked the Cantril best-possible-life question, they scored much lower than the world average. That suggests that while they may be naturally cheerful and happy, when the question is posed in relative terms and global standards come to mind, they are much more realistic.

It is possible, therefore, to come to different conclusions about the Easterlin paradox simply because of the methodology adopted—for example, what sample of countries and which happiness questions are used. The substantive question of the factors other than income that make people happy is an additional and more complicated part of the story. Some of the factors, such as public goods, are associated with income. Others, such as cultural differences in the way that people answer surveys, are not.

The chart in figure 1-1 is based on an open-ended life satisfaction question and a very simple linear specification of income (adjusted for purchasing power parity). While the richer countries are, on average, happier than the poorer ones, there is no clear income and happiness relationship *within* each set of countries, making it impossible to draw a clear conclusion about the Easterlin paradox. Figure 1-1 drums home the point that wealthier countries are, on average, happier than destitute ones, but after that, the story becomes more complicated. Country averages are influenced, among other things, by cultural differences in the way that people answer surveys, and those differences cannot controlled for in the cross-country comparisons in the way that they are when we assess happiness across large samples of individuals within and across countries.

To complicate matters further, if we were to show the same figure with a logarithmic specification of the income variable—a specification commonly used by economists that depicts income differences as proportional to the absolute size of incomes—the relationship between income and happiness would then show a much closer fit. The logarithmic specification emphasizes the importance of changes for countries with lower levels of income. Therefore, in addition to which happiness question is used, the choice of the specification of the income variable also influences the relationship between income and happiness. Little wonder that there is a great deal of debate about the Easterlin paradox (and, of course, economists would never shy away from a good debate).

HAPPY PEASANTS, FRUSTRATED ACHIEVERS, AND THE ADAPTATION CONUNDRUM

While there are clearly stable patterns in the determinants of happiness worldwide, there is also a remarkable human capacity to adapt to both prosperity and adversity. Therefore people in Afghanistan are as happy as Latin Americans—happier than the world average—and Kenyans are as satisfied with their health care as Americans. Crime makes people unhappy, but the more of it there is, the less it matters to happiness; the same goes for corruption. Obese people are less unhappy when the people around them also are obese. Freedom and democracy make people happy, but the less common those conditions are, the less they matter to happiness. The bottom line is that people can adapt to tremendous adversity and retain their natural cheerfulness, while they can also have virtually everything—including good health—and be miserable.

In contrast, one thing that people have a hard time adapting to is uncertainty. My most recent research—with Soumya Chattopadhyay and Mario Picon—shows that average happiness in the United States declined significantly as the Dow fell with the onset of the recent financial crisis. Yet when the market bottomed out and some semblance of stability was restored in March 2009, average happiness levels recovered much faster than the Dow. By June 2009 average happiness levels were *higher* than their pre-crisis levels, and they have remained higher since then—even though living standards and reported satisfaction with those standards remained markedly lower than they were prior to the crisis. Once the period of extreme uncertainty ended, people returned to their previous happiness levels, while apparently making do with less wealth (these findings are discussed in detail in chapter 4).

An analog to adaptation to lower living standards is what Eduardo Lora and I have called the "paradox of unhappy growth." In that case, we found that respondents in countries with higher growth rates were, on average, less happy than those in countries with lower growth rates, once average levels of per capita GNP were accounted for (it is important to distinguish between levels and changes in per capita GNP here: people were, on average, happier in countries with higher levels of per capita income). One explanation for our findings is found in the increases in instability and inequality that often accompany economic growth booms.

Indeed, people seem to be better at adapting to unpleasant certainty than they are to uncertainty. The capacity to adapt may be a very good thing from the perspective of the psychological well-being of the individual: for example, that of the majority of Americans who have been able to adapt to the economic costs of the financial crisis and return to their natural happiness levels, or of the average person in Afghanistan, who can maintain cheerfulness and hope despite the situation in which he or she lives. Yet that same capacity may also result in collective tolerance for conditions that would be unacceptable by most people's standards. Indeed, it may help explain why different societies tolerate such different norms of health, crime, and governance, both within and across countries.

This capacity to adapt—and the mediating role of norms and expectations—poses all sorts of measurement and comparison challenges—particularly in the study of the relationship between happiness and income. One issue, noted above, is the difficulty in comparing the happiness levels of destitute peasants with low expectations with those of very wealthy respondents with much higher expectations and awareness.

This is something that I call the happy peasant and frustrated achiever (or miserable millionaire) problem. On one level it suggests that happiness is all relative. On another it suggests that some unhappiness may be necessary to achieve economic and other sorts of progress. The examples of migrants who leave their home countries—and families—to provide better futures for their children or of revolutionaries who sacrifice their lives for the broader public good come to mind, among others.[39] This also begs more difficult questions, such as whether we should tell a poor peasant in India how miserable he or she is according to objective income measures in order to encourage the peasant to seek a "better" life—in effect telling a peasant what will make her happy. It also raises the question of whether we worry more about addressing the millionaire's misery or increasing the peasant's happiness.

This happy peasant and miserable millionaire paradox also raises the question of the appropriate definition of happiness. What makes happiness surveys such a useful research tool is their open-endedness. The definition of happiness is left up to the respondent, and we do not impose a U.S. conception of happiness on Chinese respondents or a Chinese definition on Chilean ones. The open-ended nature of the definition results in the consistent patterns in the basic explanatory variables across respondents worldwide and in turn allows us to control for those variables and to explore variance in the effects on happiness of all sorts of other things, ranging from crime rates to commuting time to the nature of governing regimes.

Yet, as noted above, "happiness" is a catch-all term that is often used to encompass various definitions of well-being, including well-being as an overall evaluation of one's life; well-being as experienced in day-to-day living; well-being as influenced by innate character traits such as positive and negative affect; and well-being as quality of life broadly defined. Those of us who study happiness go to great pains to clarify which of the various components of well-being is the focus of inquiry and select survey questions accordingly. The particular definition of interest—and the "happiness" question that is chosen—can matter a great deal to the relative importance of some critical variables of interest, in particular income, in the empirical results. That definition will also be critical to any discussion of happiness in the policy arena.

BENTHAM OR ARISTOTLE AT THE CENSUS BUREAU?

Clarity in the definition of happiness is essential to our ability to conceptualize it as a policy objective or as a measure of progress. Are we thinking of happiness as contentment in the Benthamite sense or as a fulfilling life in the Aristotelian sense? There is still much room for debate. My research suggests that respondents' conceptions of happiness vary according to their norms, expectations, and ability to adapt, among other things.

Our priors as economists and policymakers likely suggest that some conceptions of happiness—such as the opportunity to lead a fulfilling life—are worth pursuing as policy objectives, while others—such as contentment alone—are not. The libertarian paternalist approach presented by Thaler and Sunstein, which suggests that policymakers can and should "nudge" individuals in particular directions, in part by how they present or frame policy choices, is plausible. Perhaps a middle ground can be found between leaving the peasant ignorant and likely to lead a life that is by most definitions "nasty, brutish, and short" and going the "nudge" route, but finding that middle ground entails making normative judgments and engaging in a public debate that we have not yet had.

It also is plausible that people with agency or the capacity to lead fulfilling lives are more likely to emphasize the personal agency dimension of happiness or well-being, while those without agency may be more likely to find simple contentment in day-to-day living. The process of acquiring agency or opportunity, which can be facilitated by policy, may in and of itself entail unhappiness in the short term—therein the frustrated achievers versus the happy peasants. (I discuss the agency question in detail in chapter 2.) There are all sorts of policy objectives that aim to increase opportunity and aggregate welfare in the long term—ranging from reducing unsustainable fiscal deficits to reforming our health and education systems—which do not bring happiness to mind, at least not in the short term. Yet the same objectives may go a long way toward enhancing our children's happiness, quality of life, and ability to make choices in the long term.

Finally, while it is surely important to be careful before delving too quickly into the policy realm, there may be a built-in safety valve. In contrast to much philosophical work that is *prescriptive* by nature—emphasizing duty, for example—happiness surveys and the conclusions that can be drawn from them are by their very nature *descriptive*.[40] Happiness surveys help us identify the factors that make people happy. They do not, by definition, prescribe that people adopt one or more of those factors—indeed, it is not clear that they are able to. Can unhappy people without friends or a partner just go out and make friends and get married, for example? Therefore, while policymakers could—at their risk—choose to make prescriptions based on the results of these surveys, they could also simply use the information therein as inputs into the broader framework for policy design and decisions. The discussion of *how* to use happiness measures is as important to policy as the discussion of *what* measures to use.

I have introduced the question of happiness and policy cautiously, highlighting the many difficult and unresolved questions pertaining to the study of happiness and to its application to policy. Yet it is equally important to emphasize that this book is a celebration of a new science that has recently come into its own. As in any science, those of us involved in it are working hard to get the details right, to improve the robustness of the results, and to address the unanswered questions. It will, no doubt, be a work that entails trial and error. Yet it has great potential to broaden and deepen the manner in which we conceive of and measure human welfare and well-being and to inform the design of public policies intended to enhance it.

CHAPTER TWO

WHAT WE MEAN BY HAPPINESS: A "THEORY" OF AGENCY AND WELL-BEING

Pretty well most people are agreed what to call it: both ordinary people and people of quality say "happiness," and suppose that living well and doing well are the same thing as being happy. But they are in dispute about what happiness actually is, and ordinary people do not give the same answer as intellectuals.

—Aristotle, *Nicomachean Ethics*

AS THE DISCUSSION OF HAPPINESS moves from empirical studies that aim to deepen our understanding of the determinants of human well-being to happiness as a metric of economic progress or as a policy objective, it begs the question of what happiness means. That is obviously too large a question to be resolved by any one discus-

This chapter benefited tremendously from comments by Angus Deaton, Charles Kenny, and Peyton Young, as well as from the author's participation in a National Academy of Sciences workshop on national well-being indicators and the comments made there of Paul Dolan, Danny Kahneman, Richard Layard, Richard Lucas, Amanda Rowlett, David Halpern, Felicia Huppert, Becky Blank, and Bob Groves, among others. It also benefited from the comments of Jack Knight and Tom Cristiano and other participants at a conference for a special issue of *Philosophy, Politics, and Economics* in March 2011.

sion, scholar, or academic debate. But before happiness becomes a subject of policy, there are many parts of that question that merit further discussion. Foremost among them is what definition of happiness is most relevant and appropriate to apply in making policy—and how that definition varies across different societies.

That need for definitional clarity, in turn, raises some conceptual challenges for those of us who rely on happiness surveys as a research tool—and as a new microscope for examining and understanding the determinants of human well-being. As researchers, we do not define happiness for the respondent. One feature of happiness surveys that makes them a powerful research tool—and one that we can use to compare respondents in countries as diverse as Chile, China, the United States, and Afghanistan—is their open-ended nature. In other words, we do not define happiness for the respondent; each respondent defines happiness for him- or herself. Yet trying to achieve an open-ended notion of happiness does not seem to be a suitable policy objective. This chapter attempts to address that challenge and in doing so suggests a theory of how agency—for example, human capabilities and capacity—affects which definition of happiness matters most across diverse individuals and societies.

For the purposes of empirical research, leaving the definition of happiness up to the individual respondent avoids biasing the responses by introducing cultural or language differences in framing the question, among others. We simply rely on an open-ended question, which is placed at the beginning of the survey to avoid to the extent possible bias in the responses that comes from other questions, such as those about income, employment status, or health. The questions are typically "Generally speaking, how happy are you with your life?" or "How satisfied are you with your life," with possible answers ranging on a scale from "not at all" to "very" happy or satisfied. More recently, the Gallup organization has included the Cantril best-possible-life question in its worldwide poll. As a result, many scholars are conducting extensive research on well-being (which surely relates to happiness but is not the same thing, as discussed in chapter 1 and below) based on that question.

We then compare how happiness varies in relation to the variables that we are able to gather information about, such as the respondent's income, marital status, age, residence (urban/rural), employment status, and so on. The patterns that we find are remarkably consistent across respondents worldwide, including in countries at very different levels of development, in part because of the importance of these basic variables to the happiness—broadly defined—of all individuals. The open-ended nature of the happiness and life satisfaction questions does not require more fine-grained definitions from respondents, which would likely reflect cultural differences.

That consistency in patterns allows us to test for the effects of other variables, such as living under different inflation rates, kinds of government, and environmental conditions. We do not ask respondents if phenomena such as inflation, the nature of their government, pollution, and/or commuting time make them unhappy. Instead, once we have controlled for the effects of the standard socioeconomic and demographic variables (for example, age, gender, income, employment status, and so on), we determine the effects of the additional variables on their happiness scores.

This works clearly and simply from a purely scholarly perspective. From a policy perspective, however, it is more complicated. Policy is driven by factors ranging from ethical norms to aggregate welfare objectives to cultural differences. Those factors, in turn, influence the definition of happiness across individuals and countries.

Even from an academic perspective, we find that the choice of happiness question matters in assessing critical relationships such as that between happiness and income. The possible questions range from pure measures of affect, such as "How often did you smile yesterday" to the much more framed best-possible-life question, which introduces a relative component ("What is the best possible life you can imagine? How does your life compare to that life on a 10-point scale?"). A number of scholars—including me—find that income correlates more closely with the framed best-possible-life question than it does with open-ended happiness questions. Income correlates the least with the affect questions, such as "How often did you smile yesterday?" A clear example comes from my research in Afghanistan—cited at the end of chapter 1—where respondents scored higher than the world average on an open-ended happiness question but much lower than the world average on the best-possible-life question.

Surely the definition of happiness matters when we think of happiness as either a benchmark of economic progress or as a policy objective (and of whether either or both should be incorporated into actual policy measures and decisions). A plausible assumption is that most societies would be interested in maximizing the number of citizens who believed that they were leading purposeful lives but less concerned about how often people had smiled yesterday. Yet even that statement reflects normative priors that might not apply to all cultures and societies, some of which might emphasize the importance of contentment in day-to-day living more. And while the primary objective of academic research may be to identify and explain robust patterns in the determinants of happiness (and the variation in those patterns) and how the definition of happiness affects what makes people happy, policy should be concerned in addition with *why* people are happy or unhappy and how that might be changed. [1]

In this chapter, I review some of the more philosophical questions underlying the definition of happiness. I highlight some recent empirical findings that may help us understand why that definition varies across countries, cultures, and individuals within them. My review surely does not resolve all of those questions or the challenges associated with incorporating happiness measures into policy. However, it does highlight some challenges that are critical to economic, development, and welfare policy, which may be better informed by the incorporation of happiness into the discussion, regardless of which definition is deemed most important.

I also introduce the idea that people's conceptualizations of happiness (at least as captured by how they answer happiness questions) are to a large extent determined by their agency—for example, what sort of life they are *capable* of leading, given income, education, information, and other constraints. Much of my earlier research on happiness centered on the paradoxes presented by the empirical results from my research around the world. Foremost among those are the paradox of happy peasants and frustrated achievers (and/or millionaires), and the paradox of unhappy growth. Both paradoxes stem from a similar empirical observation: people with very little material wealth and limited opportunities often report being very happy, while people who have much more wealth and/or are in the process of obtaining higher levels of wealth often report being miserable.

This chapter approaches the same paradoxes but from a more philosophical perspective based on different conceptualizations of happiness and places them in the context of agency, choice, and self-selection. I posit, at least implicitly, that the absence of agency severely limits well-being, broadly defined as the capacity to lead a fulfilling life, even if respondents who lack agency report being happy. I hope that my maiden journey into the realm of philosophy goes one step toward explaining the paradoxes that my empirical work has identified but cannot fully explain.

It is important to recognize that the definitions themselves fall into various categories. Happiness can be discussed in an *epistemological* way—for example, how we obtain knowledge about happiness. This approach was, for the most part, the focus of my book *Happiness around the World*, in which I established that the basic determinants of happiness were remarkably similar across countries and cultures, regardless of development level. I also found that humans have an amazing capacity to adapt to both prosperity and adversity and maintain relatively similar levels of happiness.[2] Happiness can also be discussed or conceived of in a *prescriptive* way—for example, as a moral value or policy objective. My earlier work focused on some of the promises—and pitfalls—of this approach; this book takes that question head on. This chapter focuses on how and why an extensive discussion of the various definitions of happiness is central to pursuing such an approach.

Finally, happiness can be discussed in an *ontological* way— for example, by assessing the differences in happiness as people *evaluate* it in general terms and as people *experience* it. While this chapter only touches on this dimension, it is informed by much fine work by a number of psychologists on the topic of how people experience happiness.[3] Policymakers are likely to be more interested in—as well as able to influence—the former (how people conceive of happiness over their lifetime) than in happiness in the sense of day-to-day moments of happiness. Policy is more likely to influence the choices that underlie lifetime achievements and experiences—or provide opportunities for those choices— than those driven by momentary emotional states. Those choices, in turn, are influenced by societal norms, values, and frames, which vary across different countries and cultures.

I approach these questions with the economist's analytical frame, focusing on how individual choices result in different aggregate welfare outcomes. I then use that frame, applied to aggregate happiness outcomes, to explore how individual choices—or lack thereof—influence the nature of societies. Happiness as defined by a majority of happy peasants would lead to a society that looked very different from one in which it was defined by Aristotelians seeking purpose and virtue, for example. And different individuals would be happier living in one or the other, depending on their conception of happiness. Clarity about the different conceptualizations of happiness and which are appropriate for policy and which are not is therefore critical to the discussion of the relevance of happiness to policy.

ARISTOTLE VERSUS BENTHAM

Happiness was a subject of philosophical thought long before it entered the purview of economists or psychologists. Still, some of the earliest economists, such as Adam Smith, were concerned with happiness, and even the most parsimonious definitions of utility that underlie modern economic analysis have, as a deeper basis, some concept of individual welfare and well-being, which in turn relates to happiness. Yet the conceptualizations of happiness that are most useful in thinking about its application to policy today go much further back, to Aristotle and to Bentham.

Jeremy Bentham's concept of welfare was hedonic utility: maximizing the contentment and pleasure of the greatest number of individuals as they experienced their lives. Aristotle, on the other hand, thought of happiness as *eudaimonia*, a Greek word that combined two concepts: "eu," meaning well-being or abundance, and "daimon," meaning the power controlling an individual's destiny. The word more generally translates as "flourishing," "well-being," and/or "success."[4] In the broader life-evaluation sense, one can think of it as the opportunity to lead a purposeful or meaningful life; that is how I choose to think of it for the purposes of this discussion.

It is important to recognize that this discussion is based on how I (a rogue economist delving into the philosopher's world) choose to use the concepts of both Bentham and Aristotle. I use these concepts as an analytical frame that helps explains paradoxes in my empirical research. All errors are mine; they surely should not be attributed to Bentham or Aristotle.

For example, in Aristotle's case, it is not obvious that he conceived of *eudaimonia* as something that could be captured in what people *said* about their lives or life satisfaction. Instead, he thought of it as something that was demonstrated by how people *lived* their lives. Of course, at the time that Aristotle wrote *Nicomachean Ethics,* there were neither the large-scale surveys of what people say about their well-being nor the econometric techniques that we currently have to analyze them.

Aristotle's deeper concept of happiness was influenced by the work of others, including that of his own mentor, Plato. Plato described happiness as something that is unique because we do not want it for the sake of anything else. It is a "persistent state that emerges from devotion to wisdom and virtue."[5]

The ancient Stoics' version of happiness, while slightly different, shared the same sense of self-contentment as a persistent emotional state. They thought of happiness as something that endured over one's entire life. While they were attuned to its subjective dimensions—such as joy, euphoria, and delight—and to different agents' interior states (what we call "affect" today), they did not allow those dimensions to have a part in what they saw as "true" happiness, which was the highest good and perfection. Anyone who is happy lacks nothing, in the view of the Stoics.[6]

Epicurus, in contrast, could not conceive of anything being good if it was removed from the pleasures perceived through the senses—pleasures such as food, sex, and music, which generated sensation in the person as a whole. At the same time, he thought of happy people as self-sufficient. A happy person who is hungry and has bread but no cheese, for example, will adapt so that he wants only bread. So, rather ironically, like the Stoics, Epicureans also thought of happiness as a state of being and not just as an ephemeral experience.[7]

John Rawls, whose writings on equity and opportunity have influenced the thinking of many authors (including me), took a very different position on happiness. He defined happiness not only as pursuing a purposeful life but also fulfilling it: "Someone is happy when his plans are going well, his most important aspirations being fulfilled, and he feels sure that his good fortune will endure." In her recent book, Sisela Bok counters that view as needlessly restrictive and dependent on luck and people's ability to maintain a long time horizon. These different views indirectly speak to the happy peasant and frustrated achiever dichotomy and to the role of agency or lack thereof in helping to explain it.[8] Rawls, it seems, would not have been comfortable with labeling the happy peasant's contentment as happiness, regardless of whether the happy peasant had the capacity to live otherwise.

Descartes made a fundamental distinction between things that depend on us, like virtue and wisdom, and those that may not, such as honors, riches, and health. In an interesting twist on the question of happiness as contentment or life purpose, Descartes believed that those who were not only wise and virtuous but also favored by fortune had a greater *capacity* for contentment.[9]

More recently, a number of scholars have written about happiness as being composed of two or more dimensions, which I am roughly labeling Benthamite and Aristotelian. These dimensions are pleasure and meaning and/or hedonic utility and life evaluation. In my own work, they are embodied in the happy peasants and frustrated achievers. Kenny and Kenny also define happiness along these lines but in a broader manner: as contentment, welfare, and dignity.[10] Contentment is the cognitive evaluation that is captured by life satisfaction questions, for example. Welfare is equivalent to basic needs such as food and shelter. Dignity, the most complex of their three dimensions, entails autonomy—having control over one's life, living a meaningful life, and having respect and privilege—and corresponds most to happiness in the Aristotelian sense.

Detailed empirical work based on daily reconstruction methods by White and Dolan suggests that people may make these distinctions as they evaluate their own activities. They find that people distinguish between activities that they find pleasurable and those that they find rewarding. Time spent with children is more rewarding than pleasurable, for example, while time spent watching television is more pleasurable than rewarding.[11]

Two new studies have found important distinctions in the correlation between income and happiness, depending on which of the dimensions is studied. Diener and colleagues, in a study based on 136,000 respondents across 132 nations in the Gallup World Poll, find that income is strongly correlated with how people evaluate their lives, based on the ladder-of-life question, but only moderately correlated with day-to-day positive feelings such as those indicated by smiling.[12]

Kahneman and Deaton, in a study of 450,000 respondents in the Gallup-Healthways Well-Being Index, a daily survey of U.S. respondents from 2008 to 2009, also used the ladder-of-life question and asked questions about emotional experiences the previous day.[13] They found that hedonic well-being (the emotional quality of an individual's everyday experiences) correlated less closely with income than did life evaluation (the thoughts that people have about their life when they think about it) as measured by the ladder-of-life question. Both questions correlated closely with income (in a log-linear manner) at the bottom end of the income ladder, but the correlation between hedonic well-being and income tapered off at about $75,000 a year while the one between life evaluation and income did not.

Thus more money does not necessarily buy more happiness, but less money is associated with emotional pain. Navigating emotional challenges like divorce, anger, and depression is likely made even more difficult by having insufficient resources. At the same time, beyond a certain level, increases in income no longer improve people's ability to do what matters most to their emotional well-being. These findings highlight the importance of the distinction between the judgments that people make when they think about their life and the feelings that they experience as they live it. That the former are more sensitive to socioeconomic status is not surprising because the kinds of achievements that influence life evaluations typically hinge on means, capacity, and agency. The latter are more sensitive to circumstances that may provoke positive or negative emotions, such as spending time with friends or caring for a sick relative—circumstances that are generic to most people's lives, regardless of socioeconomic status.

Dolan makes the point that to accurately and fully measure well-being, it is necessary to capture the entire range of dimensions by relying on five separate questions: the ladder-of-life question, the life satisfaction question, two questions to measure experienced utility (for example, both positive affect, as indicated by smiling, and negative affect, as indicated by worry), and a question that captures life purpose, or *eudaimonia*. How to translate that range of questions into a metric or index that can be used in policymaking is an additional challenge and would likely require attaching relative weights to the various components, such as life purpose. Kahneman, for example, finds that questions about worry correlate very closely with issues that are of central concern to health policy (based on the Gallup Healthways survey for the United States). A much higher percentage of those without health insurance reported worrying the previous day than did those with insurance. And even more of those who were ill reported worrying.[14]

Some related findings highlight how context influences the definition of happiness that people emphasize or value. Diener and colleagues find that religion matters more to happiness in poor countries and to poor people in rich countries (where religion matters less in general) and that how the country is doing and the overall country happiness level matter more in poor countries in general and matter less to people with more personal means (health, wealth, work, and so forth) across countries.[15]

Those results accord with findings that Eduardo Lora and I obtained for Latin America.[16] We found that friends and family (who provide a safety net as well as companionship) matter more to the happiness of the poor, while work and health, which are strong determinants of an individual's capacity to get ahead, matter more to the happiness of the rich. That is not surprising; the rich tend to have more personal means, wherewithal, and capacity to lead fulfilling and purposeful lives, while the poor are more concerned with day-to-day survival. The former are therefore less dependent on communal arrangements for risk sharing and as a result may also value companionship less than the poor.[17]

Amartya Sen has repeatedly criticized the happiness literature for not taking capabilities into account:

> If someone has the power to make a difference that he or she can see will reduce injustice in the world, then there is a strong and reasoned argument for doing just that. . . . I will concentrate on the relevance of capability in the assessment of personal states and advantages, in contrast with the perspective of happiness emphasized in traditional welfare economics.[18]

Sen's capabilities approach has surely contributed enormously to our understanding of poverty. Yet I would argue that better understanding of people's different definitions of happiness can yield deep insights into their capabilities—both real and perceived. I would also argue that happiness research is hardly tied to traditional approaches in economics at all. Indeed, most harsh critics argue that it is too much of a departure!

All of these findings suggest that both dimensions of happiness matter but that which dimension matters is, at least in part, determined by an individual's capacity to pursue a purposeful and fulfilling life. In the absence of that capacity, people may place more value on day-to-day experiences, such as interactions with friends and religious experiences, while those with more capacity have less time and interest in day-to-day experiences, particularly if they are very focused on achieving some overarching goal. Some of that balance may also be determined by how people are wired genetically and respond neurologically to different kinds of stimulus.[19] A recent paper by DeNeve, Christakis, Fowler, and Frey finds that 33 percent of the variation in happiness is explained by genes, and the authors cite work by others showing that a gene-environment interaction mediates the effects of life stress on depression.[20]

These response mechanisms, meanwhile, can evolve over time and across societies depending on what sort of shared experiences particular cohorts or cultures have. At the extremes, they can produce results ranging from addiction to contentment, either because there are no opportunities for achievement and/or because addiction is too powerful to reverse. The high rates of alcoholism and related problems on Indian reservations in the United States come to mind, among others.[21] On the other side of the equation, the rich are notorious for jumping onto a hedonic treadmill in search of more money and losing sight of the importance of things like leisure time and companionship.

It is important to note that causality could run in the other direction (or in both). Happier people may value income and/or education less because they need less of it to make them happy. For example, a recent study based on longitudinal data for the same individuals in Britain finds that the higher people are on the happiness scale, the less important income is to their happiness—at least as measured by the relative weights of coefficients in econometric equations.[22]

The results suggest that within a similar context, people who already are naturally happy are influenced much less by their environment than are people who are less happy by nature, who may emphasize or seek happiness in material things, such as money. Some related work on inequality suggests that while inequality and relative income differences cause unhappiness in some contexts, it may also be that naturally less happy people are more concerned about relative income differences regardless of the context.[23]

Therefore naturally happy people who live in a deprived environment are more likely to make do and be happy with very little than are their less happy counterparts. However, an unanswered question that relates to the relationship between happiness and change or progress is whether the latter—the unhappy—are more likely to migrate to seek better opportunities elsewhere, to protest their circumstances, or to otherwise challenge the system. Those activities, while likely to produce unhappiness in the short term, may improve aggregate welfare in the longer term.

Naturally happy people who live in wealthier contexts may be more likely to select into occupations such as the arts, academia, or public service, in which success often is measured in rewards other than income, rather than into professions that emphasize monetary rewards. The British study mentioned above found that education was positively correlated with happiness in general but negatively correlated with the happiness of those on the highest end of the happiness distribution.[24] It could be that in deprived conditions, education plays a role in bursting the "bubble" of the happy peasants—for example, by raising their awareness of their lack of agency. Alternatively, in more privileged contexts, the very educated may have ambitions that are more difficult to fulfill, making even their already high levels of agency seem insufficient to make them happy.

That begs the question of whether "too much" agency results in misdirected goals, too much competition, and so forth, ultimately reducing happiness. More simply put, while some wealth, some choice, and some opportunity are good, too much may detract from happiness. A related issue is the extent to which high levels of happiness reduce the desire to compete and succeed, the extreme interpretation being that happiness is bad for progress. The happy peasants and the frustrated achievers in my research beg the same uncomfortable question.

While this is a difficult question to answer definitively, it is hard to imagine that there is a higher distribution of naturally happy people among peasants and/or people with limited agency and that happiness has been the root of their demise. Instead, it is likely that the distribution of innate happiness is relatively similar across all cohorts, societies, and cultures, albeit with some differences, and that those who are naturally happy within those distributions are better able to adapt to their environment and thus to the kind of happiness that is available to them. That suggests that, *at least on average*, most people would gain happiness from the opportunity to pursue a fulfilling and purposeful life if and when it is available.

New work along these lines by Headey and colleagues, based on the German Socio-Economic Panel, is suggestive.[25] They test whether choices—about lifestyle, work-leisure trade-offs, life partners, and socializing, for example—affect happiness over the long term. They find that giving priority to family time and altruistic activities *along with* other goals such as personal success; working as much time as (not more or less than) one desires; living with a non-neurotic partner; and choosing to socialize all are associated with higher levels of happiness. Making changes in those domains, over time, also is associated with increases or decreases in happiness.[26]

Their work not only adds to the evidence that challenges the set-point theory of happiness but also highlights the extent to which the capacity to make choices and act on them—agency—is associated with higher levels of life satisfaction. The Headey study does not have data on experienced life satisfaction (hedonic utility). Yet it is very likely that the process of making changes in any of these domains might be associated with a short-term decline in experienced life satisfaction, while having a positive impact on life evaluation over the long term. That distinction is, indeed, quite central to the broader question of what dimension of happiness "we" (in the sense of policymakers concerned with the welfare of society in the aggregate) care most about.

This over-time dimension of happiness has not been fully resolved in the literature. For research purposes, we can study happiness in several time dimensions as well as the variance between or among them. Kahneman, for example, makes a distinction in his research between day-to-day experienced utility and happiness as evaluated over the life course and measures things like pleasure and pain as distinct from life satisfaction over time. That indeed works from a measurement perspective, but from a policy perspective, should we give priority to one or another of other dimensions of happiness?

Answering these questions more definitively requires collecting data on the same people over time across a wide range of countries and cultures, as well as experimental data. Short of that, it is evident that personality traits and the environment intersect in determining what dimension of happiness matters most to people and that two-way causality is likely at play. From this author's perspective, without the benefits of the results of the proposed research in hand, happiness as evaluated over the life course, in a *eudaimonic* sense, seems a more appropriate policy objective.

EXPERIENCED WELL-BEING VERSUS EXPECTED WELL-BEING

James Ott distinguishes happiness from utility, economists' more conventional measure of welfare. He describes happiness as experienced well-being and utility as expected well-being. Happiness depends on available market and nonmarket commodities and living conditions while utility depends on available market commodities. Happiness is limited because it relates to a limited number of needs, while utility is unlimited because behavior always reveals preferences in terms of expected well-being. Needs are universal; wants vary across cultures.

Ott's depiction is useful but does not encompass the broader conceptualization of happiness in the Aristotelian or life evaluation sense. Surely happiness in the sense of hedonic utility is to a large extent determined by the fulfillment of needs: the need for sufficient food and clothing; for good health; for companionship and friendship; and so on. And those needs are, for the most part, universal. Even so, my research shows that with the exception of very basic needs, how much fulfillment of those needs matters depends to some extent on what people are used to. People are much less bothered by bad health, for example, where bad health is the norm. Respondents in Guatemala are more satisfied with their health than those in Chile, even though objective health conditions are at sub-Saharan African levels in the former and at OECD levels in the latter. Respondents in Kenya, meanwhile, are as satisfied with their health care as respondents in the United States.[27]

Therefore even hedonic utility has a relative or normative dimension to it—and surely happiness in the life evaluation sense does. Agency varies a great deal across individuals and countries. Their *capacity* to lead a fulfilling life determines in part the importance of that dimension of happiness to particular individuals as well as to their definition of a fulfilling life. This also is relevant to Ott's definition of utility. Wants also depend on agency: you want because you *can* want. That requires knowledge of what is available and some sense that what you want could be in your grasp. Expected utility more broadly defined may not be all that different from happiness in the life evaluation sense. People who aim to lead purposeful lives because they are *able to* may, in turn, also be better able to make intertemporal choices, such as sacrificing current consumption to invest in their own and in their children's education.

My research from around the world shows that people with higher prospects of upward mobility, for example, are much more likely to invest in their own and in their children's future—for example, by saving and by adopting good health practices—while people with lower expectations for the future are less likely to make such investments and therefore have higher discount rates. In contrasting but analogous findings, my work on obesity in the United States with Andrew Felton finds that the obese have lower happiness levels and lower levels of income mobility, on average, than the non-obese.[28] Their incentives for making the difficult intertemporal choices that reversing obesity would take, therefore, are much lower. The obese are much less unhappy when they are in a cohort in which obesity is the norm and in which they have less incentive to reverse the condition.

In contexts in which expectations for the future are low and discount rates are high, one can imagine that hedonic utility rather than expected utility plays a stronger role in determining happiness. That does not mean, however, that happiness in the broader life evaluation sense is not important; it just means that it is emphasized less because opportunities are fewer and expectations are lower. Making it possible for more members of a society to experience happiness in a broader life evaluation sense may be precisely where policy can play a role. Regardless of the answer to the policy question, this dichotomy clearly affects how people answer questions about their subjective well-being.

AGENCY, CHOICE, AND SELF-SELECTION: HAPPY PEASANTS AND FRUSTRATED ACHIEVERS

Surely all of the dimensions discussed matter to happiness in general, to its definition, and to the weight that different individuals place on its different dimensions. Happiness is a complex concept and a more complicated one than income, which is why, despite the limitations of income as a measure, we can not simply toss it out and replace it with happiness. The critical relationship between agency and happiness is mediated by income, among many other variables; at minimum, those who are deprived of income often lack agency as well.

At some level, the selection into different dimensions of happiness is driven by character traits. Highly driven "type A" personalities may enjoy the events of each day less but get more satisfaction out of their overall life; less ambitious people may enjoy day-to-day living more and worry less about their overall life. Yet capabilities, context, and the environment also play a major role. Expectations are driven by what people are exposed to and experience. Behavioral and consumption choices often are influenced by how choices are framed—and by whether choices are available.[29] If choices and opportunities—for example, agency—are lacking, then individuals may select into happiness in the day-to-day living sense by default, regardless of differences in character traits. We cannot, however, infer how much they would have emphasized (or not) the importance of leading a fulfilling life if had they had the opportunity to do so.

> To judge the well-being of a person based exclusively on happiness or desire-fulfillment has obvious limitations. These limitations are particularly damaging in the context of inter-personal comparisons of well-being, since the extent of happiness depends on what one can expect and how the social deal seems in comparison with that. A person who has had a life of misfortune, and very little opportunities, and rather little hope, may be more reconciled to deprivations than a person who is raised in more fortunate and affluent circumstances. . . . The hopeless beggar, the precarious landless laborer, the dominated housewife . . . may all take pleasure in small mercies and suppress intense suffering for the necessity of continuing survival, but it would be ethically deeply mistaken to attach a correspondingly small value to the loss of their well-being because of this survival strategy.[30]

Cultural differences and attitudes about mobility, opportunity, and individual effort versus collective responsibility also play a role. Americans are notorious for emphasizing individual effort; Europeans typically place more stock in collective welfare arrangements. In a comparison of Danes and Americans, Diener and colleagues found that Danes outscored Americans on both life satisfaction and best-possible-life questions and that Americans seemed to have more extreme emotional reactions, both positive and negative, than Danes did.[31] And while rich Americans and Danes are equally happy, poor Danes are happier than poor Americans—perhaps in part because the greater emphasis placed on collective responsibility and the availability of public safety nets result in less stigma associated with income poverty.

Studies of the unhappiness of the unemployed corroborate these findings on poverty-related stigma: the unemployed are less unhappy when there are more unemployed around them and when there is public support for unemployment benefits (regardless of the level of benefits). Clark and Oswald, in a study of the unemployed in Britain, found that unemployed individuals were happier in regions with higher unemployment rates. They also found that the unemployed were happier in households where there was another unemployed family member present. Stutzer, in a study comparing Swiss cantons, found that the unemployed were happier in cantons that had voted in favor of raising unemployment benefits. Andrew Eggers, Clifford Gaddy, and I found that in Russia, both the unemployed and the precariously employed are happier in regions that had higher unemployment rates (and less economic change and reform).[32]

In all of these instances, the channel seems to be that less stigma is associated with the condition—in other words, respondents can claim "It's not our fault," a claim that suggests that the issue is lack of agency (real or perceived). The stigma channel is in turn related to how much support there is for public safety nets rather than to the concerns about future employment and income that one would typically associate with higher unemployment rates.

Finally, change plays a critical role. People emphasize the dimensions of happiness that are most relevant to their lives. *Changes* in that balance, as can occur with the changes in lifestyle associated with achieving individual mobility and/or with the process of economic growth, can produce unhappiness in the short term. The paradoxes of the happy peasants and frustrated achievers and of unhappy growth that I identified at the beginning of the chapter are a case in point. The process of *acquiring agency* may in and of itself produce short-term unhappiness. And, if expectations of the prospects of a more fulfilling life are raised but the opportunity to live that life does not materialize, one can surely imagine lasting unhappiness as a result.

Some interesting related research shows that immigrants (in the United States) are less happy, controlling for all other factors, than non-immigrants. At the same time, income seems to matter more to the happiness of immigrants than non-immigrants. If one thinks of immigrants as a group of "frustrated achievers" who are trying to better their lives at some sacrifice, then both of those findings make sense: the process of acquiring agency can be painful, and during that process income gains may be more important than they are for those in more stable situations.[33] Comparison effects—for example, how their income compares with that of their new urban peers—may also be more important.

Research on the happiness of urban migrants in China provides support for that interpretation. When asked to evaluate their satisfaction with their financial situations, rural respondents, who typically are happier than urban migrants, compare their present situation with their own situation a year or so in the past. Urban migrants, in contrast, are much more likely to compare their incomes to the reference income for their new urban neighborhoods (and beyond), and they are less likely to be satisfied with their financial situation.[34]

Of course, what we do not know (and cannot know in the absence of data on the same people over time) is whether the unhappiness of migrants is simply a result of selection bias—for example, that the people who chose to migrate were unhappy in the first place and therefore more likely to choose to leave home to seek new opportunities. What we are picking up as the "unhappiness" effects of migration may well be some intersect between preexisting personality traits and whatever the effects of the change to a new environment—and new reference norms—are.

As noted above, if that is indeed the case, then the less happy respondents are also more likely to be concerned about comparisons and relative income differences.

The different definitions and components of happiness matter to key relationships, such as that between happiness and income. The work cited above by Kahneman and Deaton and by Diener and colleagues highlights how income matters more to happiness as defined in life evaluation terms than it does to happiness measured in terms of daily experiences or emotions. The importance of agency is found again in my work with Eduardo Lora on how happiness is valued in relation to friends, work, and health in Latin America. We found that while the poor place more value on their friendships, the rich place more value on work and health. The unemployment findings run along the same lines: the unemployed are unhappier about being without agency when most people around them have agency/employment.

The different components of happiness may also matter to the outcomes that happiness "causes." There are several studies that suggest that happier people are more successful in the labor market. But what component of happiness is most important to that success? Guven finds that happier people are more future oriented and less likely to engage in risky behaviors (likely because they feel that they have more to look forward to in the future).[35] Oswald, in some recent experimental work, finds that workers who have been induced to have positive rather than negative emotions (by triggers such as films) have greater intrinsic motivation and higher levels of productivity.[36]

New research by Lora and Chaparro on worker productivity in Latin America finds positive links between having meaningful work and being more productive but no significant links between job satisfaction and productivity. These findings are analogous to the life evaluation and hedonic utility dimensions of happiness. Naturally cheerful people may be more satisfied with any job than less happy people, for example, and workers with low expectations may be more satisfied with lower-quality, less productive jobs (happy peasants?). Workers who report having purposeful or meaningful work, on the other hand, are likely to have both higher expectations and higher-quality jobs. Corroborating that is the finding that informal sector workers in Latin America are more satisfied with their jobs than are formal sector workers. This may be due in part to the greater flexibility in working conditions in the informal sector, but it is also likely due to lower expectations. Andy Eggers, Sandip Sukhtankar, and I found that in Russia, happier people earn more money. The effect seems to be more important for those at lower levels of income. One can imagine that in the absence of income and its associated advantages, a good attitude is an especially important asset in the labor market (particularly in the service sector). A good attitude may still matter but is likely to be less important to workers who have other assets to leverage, such as high levels of skills and education.[37]

It may also be that people with agency are more likely to value work and therefore are more productive than those caught in a poverty trap with no prospects. The findings on the importance of work and health to the well-being of the rich and the importance of friendships to the well-being of the poor in Latin America are illustrative, as are the findings of Diener and colleagues on religion. In part, people may select into or emphasize different dimensions of happiness more because of what they are capable of—for example, agency—and in part because of inherent character traits. That may help explain the paradox of happy peasants and frustrated achievers.

It is likely positive, at least from an individual psychological perspective, that people without the agency to produce personal change can be happy with what they have. Yet in the aggregate, it may result in collective tolerance for highly negative conditions, such as those marked by high levels of crime, corruption, and poverty. My research in Afghanistan is illustrative.

As noted above, Afghans (in nonviolent areas) are happier than the world average. Again, from a psychological perspective, it seems positive that people living in such a difficult context can maintain their natural cheerfulness. Yet it is also difficult to imagine an equilibrium worse than the one in which they live, which combines high levels of crime and corruption, poor governance, prevalent poverty, and unequal gender rights. The same traits that allow people to adapt to adversity and remain happy may also result in greater tolerance for a bad equilibrium, not least because there is no immediately obvious way to change that equilibrium from the perspective of the average individual. That tolerance may result from natural cheerfulness or adaptation due to lack of agency or both. Regardless, the end result is that millions of people live in conditions that would be intolerable by most other people's standards. Sen's "hopeless beggar, precarious landless laborer, and dominated housewife" come to mind.

Our previously mentioned studies on the well-being effects of obesity in the United States also are suggestive. The obese are, on average, less happy than the nonobese. Yet they are *less unhappy* in contexts in which obesity rates are higher and the stigma associated with the condition is lower. An additional and perhaps not unrelated finding is that income mobility rates also are lower among the obese. Obesity is more likely to be the norm in low-skilled, low-mobility professions than in high-skilled professions. We do not know whether that is because obese workers make less effort in the labor market or because others discriminate against obese people or both.[38] Regardless, the condition may be contributing to poverty traps as well as to significant health problems.

People with greater prospects for upward mobility (for example, more agency) may emphasize Aristotelian (for example, life evaluation) dimensions of happiness more. A remaining question, however, is whether that quest results in as much frustration as happiness, and/or whether more or less happy people are likely to select into this pool. Our study of happiness and income in Russia as well as other psychological studies find that happier people are, on average, more likely to perform well in the labor market and to be healthier, suggesting that higher levels of happiness (and optimism about the future) lead to more effort and investment. Some psychological studies corroborate those findings. Based on a meta-analysis of 225 separate studies, Lyubomirsky, King, and Diener found that on average, happier people do better in diverse life dimensions: work, personal relationships, and health. For example, happy people receive higher job performance assessments from their supervisors, earn higher incomes, and are more likely to get married than their less happy counterparts. (There is a selection bias issue in the latter finding, however, as happy people are more likely to marry other happy people.)[39]

Yet there are limits. People who score very high on the happiness ladder (at the top of a 9-point scale) typically are the most successful in terms of close relationships and volunteer work, but they do not do as well in terms of income, education, and political participation as those who score slightly lower (7 and 8 points on the same scale).[40] Those findings may in turn reflect the different dimensions of happiness and their potential role. The Lora findings on job satisfaction are suggestive here as well—those who are simply satisfied with their jobs are not more productive than the average, while those who report having meaningful work are more productive.

To what extent are such differences driven by factors other than agency—for example, character traits and cultural context? Because those factors are interrelated, it is difficult to disentangle their effects. Attempting to change culture and character seems outside the purview of policy (unless we think that policy can or should change such things). In contrast, agency and its distribution across socioeconomic and other cohorts is surely relevant to policy.

An interesting additional perspective on that question comes from David Brooks, who has studied the role of noncognitive skills, such as emotions and parts of the unconscious mind (all of which are typically ignored by formal education systems), in determining the personal and professional success of individuals.[41] Those additional elements, while hard to identify specifically, are likely part of what constitutes agency.

This discussion in turn begs the question of whether people select into the various dimensions of happiness by *choice* (conscious or unconscious), which is in part driven by character traits, or whether they are in one or the other primarily because of their capabilities and agency. The latter, in turn, are determined by individual endowments, by the external environment, and by cultural norms. To the extent that societies and individuals within them are merely adapting to bad circumstances due to lack of choice or agency and therefore reporting themselves to be happy, there may be room for policy in helping to provide equal opportunity and agency. Yet, as the frustrated achiever findings as well as those on the unhappiness of migrants suggest, the transition from unpleasant certainty to an uncertain if more promising future can produce unhappiness, at least in the short term.

A recent experimental study, based on a sample of several hundred respondents in Britain, suggests that most people would rather have a chance to experience life and find their own happiness than take a hypothetical happy "pill" that makes them content for life. While the study was only an experiment based on a small sample, it suggests that when people are offered a hypothetical choice between lifetime contentment and establishing their own course and individual happiness, most opt for the latter.[42] Again, the latter choice may result in all sorts of frustrations even though it may produce a more fulfilling life over the long term. As I posited at the beginning of the chapter, lives that totally lack agency and the opportunity to make such choices are deprived of an important dimension of well-being. The above-cited study by Headey and colleagues, which shows that happiness can be increased or decreased depending on such choices, supports the interpretation that having and exercising agency is important to well-being.

Resolving or at least achieving better understanding of these dimensions of human well-being—and their determinants—is, in my view, an essential part of any discussion of using happiness data and benchmarks in the policy arena. It is essential because we need to clarify which dimension or dimensions of happiness (if any) should be the objective of policy. The answer is likely to vary across societies. Answering the question also raises deeper social issues—about the distribution of opportunities, about the relative effects of innate talents and the environment in determining individual capabilities, and about intertemporal priorities. Are we willing to forgo some happiness, today through fiscal sacrifices, for example, so that our children can have better educations, opportunities, and environments tomorrow? To what extent can or should policy frame public choices so that they enhance health, wealth, and happiness, as suggested by libertarian paternalism, for example?[43]

Another issue, which has been highlighted in recent work by Frey and Stutzer, is the challenges posed by aggregating results based on surveys of individual preferences into an overall societal happiness welfare function. In particular, the authors highlight how such an approach overlooks both individual incentive problems and the critical role of political institutions. They suggest that rather than thinking about the optimization of aggregate happiness as a policy goal, policymakers should use the happiness metrics and the information that the metrics provide to improve the processes through which citizens can express their preferences.[44]

Along the same lines, one can imagine happiness—and the information in happiness surveys—being misused by politicians. What makes people happy in the contentment sense, as reported in surveys, is useful information for researchers and can inform policy choices. But it could also, taken at face value or to the extreme, provide political fodder for all sorts of things, ranging from irresponsible fiscal policies to subsidies for junk food.

Take, for example, the unhappy growth paradox. We know that the changes associated with economic growth—and rapid growth in particular—make people unhappy in the short term. Yet we also know that the higher levels of income and prosperity and the associated public goods that result from growth over the long term are associated with higher levels of well-being. That finding tells us that the nature and pattern of growth matter and suggests that when possible, policy should be directed at mitigating the uncertainty and inequality related to very rapid economic growth. Yet an irresponsible politician could easily either misinterpret or misconstrue those nuances and make the case that economic growth in general is bad for happiness.

Similarly, we know that unemployment is bad for happiness but that the unemployed are less happy when there is more unemployment. Should we therefore not worry about high unemployment rates? The same goes for obesity: obese individuals are unhappy, but they are much less unhappy when there is more obesity around them. So why not promote junk food for the obese as a policy? Those examples are, of course, extreme. However, different iterations are surely possible in contexts in which enlightened despots are in control and/or in which high proportions of the population are illiterate and have very low expectations (happy peasants).

All said, the information that comes from happiness surveys provides an important complement to the limited picture of well-being that we are able to garner from income data, and it provides us with a broader and deeper base upon which to design policies. The unhappy growth paradox does not tell us to toss out economic growth; it tells us that its nature and pattern matter and that the process can be very unsettling. The obesity findings do not mean that we should promote obesity; they suggest that public health messages about the dangers of obesity may need to be tailored differently for cohorts in which obesity is the norm. And the findings on uncertainty and unpleasant certainty in general—including those from our research on the recent economic crisis in the United States, discussed in chapter 4—surely should make policymakers more aware of the positive role that different kinds of safety nets and insurance policies could play in enhancing well-being in general, without discounting the need for continued economic progress.

Resolving these questions might also contribute to economic theory by deepening our conceptualizations of welfare and utility. Utility defined simply by consumption choices equates the purchase of a Big Mac by an obese individual with that of a guitar string purchased by a professional musician. Yet the purpose of each of those choices is very different, even if each produces a form of "happiness" for the purchaser. Making that distinction surely has a normative dimension. The libertarian paternalist approach advocated by Thaler and Sunstein (neither of whom could be accused of being a traditional economist) would argue that policy should frame choices in a way that encourages better choices (on the basis of long-term health and well-being) and thus would encourage the *choice* of guitar materials over Big Macs.

While I am not advocating this approach per se, it certainly could usefully complement the information that is in happiness surveys—for example, by making individuals aware of the trade-offs involved in making choices that overemphasize hedonic utility (for example, eating Big Macs) over investing in longer-term life goals (learning to play a guitar). Yet effective public information policies along these lines would have to have a basis in an understanding of the reasons why some people—and even entire cohorts—emphasize one dimension or definition of happiness more than another. While not fully developed, this example suggests how happiness economics—along with other new approaches—can help us better understand the determinants of human welfare and in turn develop more informed policy choices.

There also is an additional normative question, which is whether policy should value experienced well-being or evaluated well-being more. In other words, should policy aim to maximize Benthamite or Aristotelian happiness more? On what basis can that decision be made? Clearly both components of well-being matter to overall happiness, although some people emphasize one more than the other, perhaps, as suggested previously, because of their agency or capabilities. Yet policy also needs to be concerned with outcomes, and we have metrics for valuing outcomes in terms of well-being. Some short-term frustration or delayed gratification often is necessary to complete certain goals, such as achieving higher levels of education or becoming a doctor (or an economist), and the negative experience component is likely outweighed by the overall contribution that achieving such goals makes to well-being in a life evaluation sense.

Therefore, as we consider which components of well-being are most appropriate for consideration by policymakers, we must also attach some sort of value to the *outcomes* that stem from experience. The positive experience that an obese person might gain from consuming several Big Macs should be evaluated in the context of the negative effects that doing so might have on that person's ability to lead a healthy and/or fulfilling life.

A more complex example is the whole issue of change and the process of acquiring agency. Fundamentally, people do not like change. Yet change, and often unsettling change, is typically necessary to achieve the kinds of progress that advance human welfare in the aggregate. The development process and the increased frustration that often accompanies increases in awareness and education are a good example. The unhappiness of migrants who go to the city hoping to provide their children a better education and other opportunities and to increase their capacity to pursue happy and fulfilling lives is a related one. (The happy peasants and frustrated achievers come to mind again). Therefore, as we consider how to approach happiness from a policy perspective and whether to focus on experienced or evaluated well-being (or hedonic utility or life satisfaction), we need to also have a metric that allows us to capture the intertemporal dimensions of well-being and the value of goals or outcomes.

Perhaps one way to frame this is to ask whether happiness *per se* or the *pursuit* of happiness should be the focus of policy. The U.S. Declaration of Independence clearly states that people have an "inalienable right" to "the pursuit of happiness." Most Americans seem to care much more about equality of *opportunity*—for example, the opportunity to pursue outcomes—than they do about equality of outcomes per se. Indeed, compared with most other societies, Americans do not seem to care about equality of outcomes at all.[45] In addition, sustainable happiness, which goes beyond simple contentment, is not a passive concept. When we conceptualize well-being and quality of life, from both the philosophical and the policy perspective, we care about what people are doing with their minds, talents, and time. A conceptual frame that seeks to maximize the capacity of the most individuals to pursue happiness and fulfillment may be the appropriate framework for beginning to think about policy. That is a subject that I will revisit in the final chapter.

CONCLUSIONS

This review of the different definitions of happiness and their relation to agency and capabilities is intended as an input to the discussion of which definitions are most appropriate for policy. It also raises a number of difficult and as yet unanswered questions.

The first is whether individuals select into distinct definitions of happiness because of agency or because of their particular personality traits. While we can show empirically that agency is likely to play a role, it is also likely that people with particular character traits may emphasize one or another dimension more. The latter possibility is much more difficult to prove empirically. For example, it may be that people who are naturally content may emphasize and enjoy day-to-day living more and therefore seek hedonic utility. Those with a tendency toward frustration *and* with the agency to evoke change may seek happiness in purposefulness and therefore may emphasize life satisfaction, even if they enjoy their day-to-day experiences less. Yet that is hard to demonstrate without detailed, longitudinal data for large samples of individuals.

At the same time, there is quite a bit of evidence that happier people perform better in the labor market and are healthier, suggesting that they have more capacity to lead purposeful lives. The psychology literature suggests that people who are on average happier also perform better but that those who score the highest on happiness actually do worse on achievement dimensions than their slightly less happy peers. It may be that some innate happiness is good and contributes to both contentment and purposefulness but that too much happiness may lead to complacency, which often is associated with inferior outcomes in the health and labor market arenas, among others.

Even if contentment is important to happiness, a more natural focus of policy is the dimensions of happiness that have to do with the opportunity to lead a purposeful life—that, at least, is my strongly normative conclusion. Whether that normative judgment would hold across U.S. society more broadly and then across societies more generally is a question that requires a more general public debate prior to introducing happiness measures into the policy domain. In the United States, that conclusion is supported by the phrasing in the Declaration of Independence, which calls for the "pursuit of happiness" rather than happiness per se. It also is supported by our clear societal preferences for policies that support equality of opportunity rather than equality of outcomes.[46]

A related question is whether we can really weigh these two dimensions of happiness against each other. While our priors may tell us that the purchase of a guitar string for a concert musician is a "better" purchase than that of a Big Mac by an obese individual, we do not have the theoretical or empirical metrics to attach cardinal weights to those two choices. This discussion may encourage us to develop the tools to do so, but we do not yet have them in hand.

This discussion also begs the question of balance. All contentment is not bad; indeed, much contentment is incredibly important to many people's happiness and to their leading fulfilling lives. A complete focus on life purpose can result in people neglecting things that are incredibly important to happiness in general, such as health and family life. It is not a coincidence that religions around the world focus on reminding people of the importance of family and friendships over material pursuits.

Finding a way to describe and understand different kinds of utility is one thing, and acting on them in policy terms is another, not least because we do not fully understand why some people emphasize one kind of utility and others emphasize another. If people make poor choices due to a lack of agency, then enhancing their agency seems a worthwhile policy objective. Yet if we do not have a complete explanation of what underlies those decisions, we can hardly justify policy actions, much less identify effective interventions.

Some recent work by Angus Deaton provides a useful analogue. Deaton notes that many new methods in economic development—such as randomized trials and other research based on experiments—can help us establish causal mechanisms more clearly: for example, that x causes y and not the other way around. Yet they still do not resolve the fundamental question of *why* something worked or why it did not—or even whether causality would work the same way in a different context. The latter remains a much broader question than the discrete interventions that experiments and trials are able to evaluate, and it applies to the larger question of why some societies develop and progress and others stay behind.[47]

The answer to the question of why people emphasize different dimensions of happiness is likely to lie in some interaction between the agency of individuals (which is exogenous due to the environment but also endogenous to genes and talents) and their innate character traits (which are endogenous). Therefore, while we may be able to establish the specific variables and their direction of causality through careful empirical and experimental work, we still may not be able to answer the fundamental question of how and why they play out differently across different individuals and societies and their overall level of happiness.

From a policy perspective, *if* we had a national debate about which kind of happiness was a worthwhile objective of national policy *and* we concluded that policy should focus on happiness in the life evaluation/Aristotelian sense rather than on hedonic utility and contentment in the Benthamite sense, then we would also need to accept that providing people with the agency to focus on the former rather than the latter could generate a fair amount of unhappiness in the short term.

That in turn would require societies to implement the kinds of policies that would increase the agency of individuals who lack it. You cannot propose that people seek happiness in a more purposeful manner without providing them the tools to do so. That would require major public investments in education and all of the other interventions that enhance opportunity. And one policy conclusion from this thought experiment could be that policy should not focus on happiness at all but on enhancing agency and opportunities that allow people to pursue happiness.

One can imagine that the worst societies, in terms of happiness and equity, would be those that were founded on or preached the ideal of equality but that did not, in fact, offer equal opportunity or agency. Rather ironically, unfulfilled promises might lead to more unhappiness or social unrest than would more traditional class- or caste-based inequality, no matter how unjust it might be. A host of studies on the links between unfulfilled expectations and revolution, among other things, provides some backing for this proposition.[48]

Perhaps one goal that a policy discussion about the different dimensions of happiness can achieve is evaluation of how preferences along these lines vary across different individuals and societies and how those preferences might be better supported by public policy. I return to this theme—albeit without resolving all of the questions that it raises—in the final chapter of the book.

CHAPTER THREE

HAPPINESS AROUND THE WORLD
What We Know

At fifteen I set my heart on learning; at thirty I took
my stand; at forty I had no delusions; at fifty I knew
the Mandate of Heaven; at sixty my ear was attuned;
at seventy I followed my heart's desire without
overstepping the boundaries of right.

Confucius, *The Analects* (2:4)

I HAVE SPENT MUCH OF the last decade studying happiness around the world, and it has surely been the most interesting enterprise that I have undertaken since I began to do research on economic development as a graduate student many years ago. In chapter 2, I identified a host of unanswered questions raised by that research. Those questions, which hinge on the definition of happiness, have led me into uncharted philosophical waters. In this chapter, I return to firmer empirical ground (at least for me) and review the regularities that I and others have found in the determinants of well-being around the world. Rather ironically, finding those regularities may hinge on not imposing a definition

This chapter draws heavily on chapter 3 in Carol Graham, *Happiness around the World: The Paradox of Happy Peasants and Miserable Millionaires* (Oxford University Press, 2009). It can be skipped by readers familiar with the literature.

of happiness at all but on using a simple, open-ended survey question about happiness.

When I began this work, most studies of happiness, both by economists and psychologists, focused on countries that had reached a certain level of economic prosperity, in particular the United States and European countries.[1] That was due to the availability of data and also to an implicit assumption that people in the developing world were too concerned with day-to-day survival to worry about the more ephemeral concept of happiness. My 2002 work on Latin America with Stefano Pettinato was the first to study happiness in a large-scale sample of developing countries. Our findings were notable in that the basic determinants of happiness were very similar to those for wealthier countries, despite the fact that most countries in our sample had much lower levels of per capita income and substantial proportions of their populations lived in subsistence-level poverty. In all countries, income clearly mattered to happiness, but other key variables such as age, marital and employment status, and health, mattered as much if not more in some instances. I have since studied happiness in a number of other developing and transition economies. Remarkably, the same patterns seem to appear.

Comparing average happiness levels across countries is by definition a difficult and imprecise exercise. Results may be driven by unobservable differences across countries and cultures as much as they are by objective measures such as economic progress, the nature of governments, and the distribution of public goods. [2] There is surely a relationship between income and happiness, with wealthier countries being, on average, happier than very poor ones. There may also be a relationship over time as very poor countries begin to get wealthier, but the effect diminishes as they move up the wealth curve. But there also are many outliers, with some very poor countries, like Nigeria, reporting extremely high happiness levels and some very wealthy ones, like Japan, having relatively low levels, which have fallen even during times of remarkable prosperity. The nature of that relationship is very much influenced by the happiness question that is used, by the countries in the sample, and by the manner in which income is measured.

The findings on the determinants of happiness *within* countries are more consistent and robust, as large cross-sections and micro-level data allow us to control for a number of factors that vary across individuals, such as age, income, gender, marital and employment status, and so on.

Virtually all within-country studies find that wealthier people are, on average, happier than poorer ones. They also find remarkable consistency in the effects of other variables, such as age (which has a U-shaped relationship with happiness, with the low point being in the mid- to late forties), marital status (marriage is good for happiness, for the most part), unemployment (bad for happiness), and health (very important to happiness).[3] (For an example of the age and happiness relationship, see figure 3-1.)

The influence on happiness of other variables—such as gender, education, and certain kinds of employment status—varies more, likely due to differences in gender rights across countries, to different returns to education as countries make structural changes at various stages of the development process, and to differences in the economic stability of the self-employed and retired, among others.[4]

While my research began in Latin America, I have examined happiness in a wide range of developing or transition economies, from Russia, Central Asia, and selected countries in Africa to Afghanistan. To the extent that we find modest differences in the determinants of happiness within countries, they are usually easily explained by major structural differences in economies and labor markets and/or by notable changes in those structures as countries make the transition from one type of economy to another.

COMPARING LATIN AMERICA, RUSSIA, AND THE OECD

The 2002 study of happiness in Latin America that Stefano Pettinato and I undertook was the first study of happiness in such

FIGURE 3-1. Happiness by Age, Latin America (2001) and United States (2008-09)

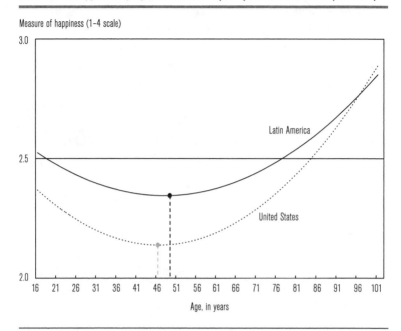

Measure of happiness (1-4 scale)

Age, in years

Source: Author's calculations with Soumya Chattopadhyay (March 2011) using Latinobaró-metro (2001) and Gallup Daily Poll (2008-09).

a large sample of developing countries and certainly the first for the region.[5] In order to see whether the determinants of happiness in the developing countries were different—and if so, how—we compared Latin American countries with the United States and Russia. Making such comparisons is rife with methodological challenges related to both cultural differences and the differences in the nature of the data sets that are available. The data set that we had for Russia, for example, was ideal because it contained panel data—data on the same respondents obtained over time by interviewing them repeatedly—which allowed us to control for individual personality traits or idiosyncrasies. The data set for the United States and Latin America contained cross-section data—data obtained each year on a set of similar, but not the same, respondents.

For Latin America, we relied on the Latinobarómetro (1997–2008) survey, which consists of approximately 1,000 annual interviews in each of eighteen countries in Latin America. The surveys, which are conducted by a prestigious research firm in each country, are nationally representative for most of the countries.[6] For the United States, we used the pooled data for 1973–98 from the General Social Survey (GSS), a nationally representative cross-section survey of approximately 30,000 Americans a year.[7] For Russia, we relied on the Russia Longitudinal Monitoring Survey (RLMS), which covered an average of almost 13,000 Russians a year from 1992 to 2001 and from which we created a set of panel data containing data from 1995 and 2000.[8] All three of the surveys used either happiness or life satisfaction questions.

Despite the potential difficulties, we found a remarkable degree of similarity across all samples, which showed similar age, income, education, marriage, employment, and health effects.[9] In all contexts, wealthier people were, on average, happier than poorer ones, although the relationship between income and happiness was not necessarily linear. That was due not only to the complex relationship between income and happiness, but also to the specification of our income variable. We used a logarithmic specification of income in our regressions, which increases the importance of income at the bottom of the scale, where it typically matters more to happiness. There is likely more variance at the top end of the income scale. Education also is positively correlated with happiness in most contexts, except in Latin America, where income and education are so closely correlated that the significance of education goes away when income is included in the regression. Marriage is positively correlated with happiness in both the United States (and in Europe, based on other studies) and Latin America. Marriage is not, however, significantly correlated with happiness in Russia (where happiness levels are generally lower and where there has been a tumultuous economic transition). Both self-reported health and objective measures of health are positively correlated with happiness in all three contexts.[10] In all contexts, unemployed people were less happy than others. On average, self-employed people were happier in the United States and in Russia but less happy in Latin America. While in the United States self-employment often is a choice, in Latin America the self-employed often work in the informal sector by default due to a shortage of stable jobs. Retired individuals were happier than average in the United States but much less happy than average in Russia; that confirms the findings of many other studies (from very different perspectives) that highlight how poorly Russian pensioners fared in the transition from a centrally controlled to an open economy. Another difference was that women were happier than men in the United States while in Russia men were happier than women (perhaps due to disparities in status) and in Latin America there was no gender difference. Blacks were less happy than other races in the United States, and similarly, those who identified themselves as minorities in Latin America were less happy. In contrast, minorities were happier than ethnic Russians, probably because the status of minorities increased in post-communist Russia and many native Russians experienced transition-related losses in income and status.[11]

We could not establish the direction of causality with our findings, particularly when we had only cross-section data. It could be that health makes people happier or that happier people are healthier. Marriage may make people happier; in contrast, happier people may marry each other.[12] We explore causality issues in greater detail in subsequent work, finding evidence that causality runs in both directions. Marriage and good health make people happier, and happier people are more likely to marry each other and to have good health.

HAPPINESS IN TRANSITION ECONOMIES:
CENTRAL ASIA, CUBA, AND EASTERN EUROPE

Central Asia, which has seen its share of political and economic turmoil in recent years, is one of the more complex places in which I have studied happiness, not least because of political repression and even revolution in one of the countries, Kyrgyzstan, around the time of our surveys. Working with a team of scholars from the United Nations Development Program (UNDP) and the World Bank, we implemented a well-being and public opinion survey of four Central Asian countries in October-November 2004. The survey was intended to help identify particular socioeconomic and political challenges facing the region. In particular, the analysis focused on potential factors driving civil unrest in the region, such as economic hardship (both real and perceived) and ethnic tensions. We included an open-ended happiness question.

The survey was implemented in Kazakhstan, Kyrgyzstan, Tajikistan, and Uzbekistan, in collaboration with local polling firms. (Surveying in Turkmenistan was not possible due to the complex political situation there.) The surveys covered 1,000 respondents per country and were, to the extent possible, nationally representative.

For the most part, we found that the respondents in Central Asia, despite the difficult context, were no different from most other populations. Income, defined by both the respondent's assessment of his or her purchasing power and the interviewer's assessment of the respondent's socioeconomic status, was an important component of happiness. Self-reported socioeconomic status and rank also mattered to happiness.

As in other populations, age had a U-shaped relationship with happiness in Central Asia, although the low point (age fifty-one years) was older than that for most OECD economies (usually in the mid-forties) and more typical of the pattern for developing economies.[13] As in the rest of the world, marriage was good for happiness and unemployment was bad for happiness.

While most of the basic patterns were similar, happiness in the region also exhibited some differences from the rest of the world, which likely reflect the rather tumultuous nature of the region's economic and political transition. In particular, a number of aspects of "social capital" in these countries do not seem to follow typical patterns. Three aspects of social capital on which Central Asia stands out from the rest of the world are trust and community involvement, ethnic relations, and religion.

As in the rest of the world, respondents who said that they trust other people, participate in community activities, and feel safe, were happier on average. In Central Asia, however, trusting others, by itself, was not correlated with happiness. While we cannot explain that finding in any definitive way, we posit that the authoritarian or semi-authoritarian nature of governments in the region may create a climate of general mistrust that diminishes at the local level, where neighbors know each other. In addition, respondents who report they can trust most individuals may be outliers for other, unobservable reasons. Answers to a question about whether the respondent feels safe walking alone at night were significantly correlated with happiness, as one would expect, providing additional evidence of differences between the interpretation of "trust" in Central Asia and in the rest of the world.

Migration in the region is high, and there is a large contingent of non–Central Asians, Russians in particular. Russians and other ethnic groups that immigrated during the Soviet period, such as Ukrainians, tended to be poorer, older, and less happy than Central Asians. Prior to the fall of communism, Russians tended to have management and other desirable positions; since then their fate has been much less favorable. Kazakh and Kyrgyz migrants, on the other hand, tended to be wealthier and happier.

In terms of reported happiness, we found that outsiders—as defined by their response to a question that asked non-natives whether their ethnicity or their citizenship matters more as well as to a question about whether they think in the native language— were less happy than others. The only place that that finding did not hold was Kyrgyzstan, where migrants were, on average, happier than others. Minorities in Kyrgyzstan were also outliers in that their perceived economic rank or position (as measured by the economic ladder question) was higher than average; perceived positions of migrants elsewhere were lower than average.

There is a diversity of religions in the region, and 95 percent of respondents reported some religious affiliation. In most countries, respondents who expressed faith or religious affiliation—as well as those who practiced their faith—were happier than others.[14] We attempted to gauge intensity of commitment and Islamic orientation by identifying respondents who prayed five times a day, who constituted 40 percent of those responding to the question. In most of the rest of the world, groups with more intense faith are happier, on average, than others. Instead, the mean happiness scores of those who prayed five times a day are almost exactly the same as the average. That may be because religion is more of a divisive force in Central Asia than in the more moderate contexts where it has been studied in depth, as in Europe.

In general, according to our social well-being measures, Central Asians are very similar to other people around the world. However, the link between happiness and social capital indicators is less strong in the region than it is most other places—perhaps no surprise for recently independent countries still forging a social contract and for contexts in which political freedom is incomplete.

CUBA

Cuba has been on the cusp of economic transition for years, while its political system remains dominated by an authoritarian regime. Yet Cubans have a popular reputation for being remarkably cheerful. The explanation that is usually given is that natural cheerfulness is prevalent among the population and/or that the population has widespread access to public health and education services.

While we did not have a national survey, we did have access to a pilot study conducted in the two largest cities in Cuba—Santiago and Havana—by Jesus Rios and Johanna Godoy of the Gallup Organization for the Gallup World Poll, an effort in which I also am involved.[15] The study polled 600 respondents in Havana and 400 in Santiago in September 2006 and compared the responses of Cuban respondents to those of other Latin American respondents in the Gallup World Poll for the same year. The results are representative of the 3 million respondents of the two cities but not for any other areas. Therefore the results reported here are just a snapshot of attitudes, and they are limited to the urban areas surveyed.

Despite Cuba's reputation as a happy country, only 62 percent of the Cubans who responded said that they had laughed or smiled the day before (the corresponding figure was to 82 percent for Latin America overall), and only 64 percent of the Cubans said that they had experienced enjoyment for much of the previous day, while approximately 80 percent of Latin Americans in general said that they had. While there was no difference in the percent of respondents who reported negative emotions (such as depression) and the average for Latin America, there clearly was less positive emotion than was typical for Latin America.

The questions related above capture positive emotion or "affect." Other questions are better suited for capturing different elements of life satisfaction. On that front, Cubans were more optimistic than the Latin American average about the quality of their public services but far less positive than average about their freedom and opportunities to determine their economic welfare. Ninety-six percent of Cubans said that health care was available to anyone, regardless of their economic situation, while 98 percent said the same about education. The Latin American averages, in contrast, were 42 percent and 52 percent respectively.

Cubans scored much lower than average on economic opportunity questions. Only 60 percent of Cubans who had a job said that they had the opportunity to do what they do best at work while the figure was 84 percent for the region as a whole. Job satisfaction also was lower: only 68 percent of Cubans but 83 percent of Latin Americans in general were satisfied with their jobs. Only 55 percent of Cubans reported having had the opportunity to decide what to do with their time the day before while 75 percent of Latin Americans were able to do so. And, most notable, only 26 percent of Cubans were satisfied with their freedom to choose what to do with their lives, a figure three times lower than the Latin American average of 80 percent.

As in the case of the Central Asian findings, the divergences from the average in Cuban well-being responses seem to be grounded in realistic assessments of what life is like in Cuba rather than in a nationally shared character trait. At the same time, because we cannot systematically compare Cuban happiness or ladder-of-life responses to those of other Latin Americans or people in the rest of the world—both because the questions differ and because the Cuban responses were from urban areas only—we must be very cautious in inferring too much from any comparisons.

It is worth thinking about the findings in Cuba in light of Richard Easterlin's findings for the transition economies of Eastern Europe, which have proceeded much further in their transition to the market economy than Cuba has but where the availability of public services has deteriorated at the same time.[16] Easterlin finds that life satisfaction in the transition economies from 1989 to 1999 followed the same V-shape pattern that GDP did in those countries but that it failed to recover commensurately. In general, increased satisfaction with material well-being has occurred at the expense of satisfaction with work, health, and family life, which has decreased. The disparities in life satisfaction were greatest for the less educated and persons over the age of thirty years; both cohorts were less able than the average to cope with the dramatic economic transition that their countries underwent. Life satisfaction in different domains seems to reflect the increase in economic opportunity that accompanied the economic transition in Eastern Europe on one hand, and the increase in insecurity on the other.

HAPPINESS IN AFRICA: OPTIMISM AMID ADVERSITY[17]

Data for Africa are very limited, in terms of both country coverage and specific happiness questions. The data that we do have are based on the Afrobarometer opinion survey, which has conducted at least one round of interviews in eleven countries in Africa.[18]

Work that Stefano Pettinato and I did on Latin America and Russia found that higher levels of optimism and happiness (variables that correlate very closely with each other) were also associated with other positive traits and behaviors, such as productivity in the labor market, better health outcomes, and higher levels of support for democracy and markets. Matthew Hoover and I used those findings as a benchmark for our look into Africa. In Africa, poverty is more widespread than in Latin America and Russia and democratic governments and market economies are very fragile, so we were able to examine well-being under some of the most extreme conditions. In the absence of a straightforward happiness question in the Afrobarometer, we chose to focus on optimism as a proxy for happiness.[19]

Our study yielded both expected and unexpected results. In terms of the former, we found that African respondents' views about improvement in their *own* economic situation in the near future were positively correlated with income, education, and other variables that are indicative of better socioeconomic status, as they are in Latin America. Yet we found that in contrast to respondents in most other places, the *poorest* respondents in Africa were the most optimistic about their *children's* future mobility. We posit that respondents' optimism about the short-term future (twelve months hence) is more closely linked to objective conditions—such as income, education, and realistic prospects—while optimism about their children's future status compared with their own is based on a much more speculative exercise that likely captures innate optimism as well as objective criteria. We repeated essentially identical equations for Latin America, based on Latinobarometro data. The results for Africa and Latin America ran in opposite directions—in Latin America, higher income was *positively* correlated with optimism for children's future, unlike in Africa.

Given our doubts about accurate income reporting, we assessed poverty in a number of different ways: by low reported income, low level of education, lack of access to health care, and higher likelihood of being a crime victim. Most of those measures were significantly and positively correlated with reported optimism for children's prospects. For example, respondents who reported that they had been a victim of a crime in the past year were more likely than the average to give a positive assessment of their children's future prospects. [20]

While we cannot establish causality, we posit that optimism may enhance the survival prospects of the poor in such adverse circumstances. These findings may also help explain how the unusual levels of optimism among the poorest and most insecure respondents depart from findings for more developed regions, where optimism is positively correlated with wealth, education, and other signs of prosperity. The results may also reflect realism on the part of the rich. In the unstable, low-growth reality of most African countries, those in the top quintiles might be making a realistic assessment that things were not likely to get materially better any time soon and that their children were not likely to live better than they did.

HAPPINESS IN AFGHANISTAN: ADAPTING TO EXTREMES

Like Africa, Afghanistan is a country in which individuals have to cope with the most adverse of circumstances. Our results once again demonstrate the remarkable consistency across countries of the determinants of happiness, even in the midst of extreme circumstances. At the same time, relatively high average happiness scores in Afghanistan are balanced by much lower scores on the best-possible-life question. That suggests that Afghans may be naturally cheerful and/or may have adapted their expectations downward in the face of adversity, yet are more realistic (or pessimistic) when thinking about their situation in relative terms.

Our survey of well-being in Afghanistan was carried out in collaboration with AIR Consulting in Kabul, in collaboration with the University of Kabul.[21] We interviewed 2,000 individuals from eight provinces in Afghanistan in January 2009. The interviews were conducted by recent graduates from the university who had received prior training in survey research through a number of international institutions. The survey was a pilot, and the results are by definition preliminary.

Provinces were chosen on the basis of the feasibility of conducting interviews, including the ability to reach them in difficult winter conditions, and the safety of the interviewers. Therefore our results come with a caveat, because we have not surveyed in the most difficult and conflict-ridden parts of the country. Still, approximately 400 of our respondents were from areas that were somewhat influenced by the Taliban. Within the provinces, individuals were drawn randomly from the whole population.[22]

The Afghan context posed some challenges. For example, although the interviewers explained the survey's purpose, most respondents were skeptical about their intentions. That is not surprising given the complex political situation in Afghanistan. Not surprisingly, we found gender issues to be a challenge. Many of the randomly selected women in the survey would not answer the questionnaire (especially in the Taliban-influenced areas). Typically they were afraid that their husbands, fathers, brothers, and other relatives would see them talking to a group of strangers. The randomly drawn women in Kabul were much more likely to answer the interviewers than were those elsewhere. That creates a selection bias in our gender findings, of course, as those who answered were likely to be much freer and more educated than the average. Cold weather and snowy roads also created obstacles to the survey process. Finally, insecurity arising from conflict in some areas and towns made interviewing much more difficult than is typical for such surveys.

Despite the obstacles and the margin of error that they introduce, our results show surprising consistency with those of happiness surveys in other contexts. Overall, mean happiness levels in Afghanistan—which were measured by the general question "How happy are you with your life?" on a scale ranging from "Not at all" to "Very" (phrased and scaled exactly as in the Latinobarometro) were relatively high. The mean happiness score for Afghanistan was 2.62, while the score for Latin America for 1997–2007 (the latest year for which we have data) was 2.8. The standard deviation in Latin America was higher (0.93 versus 0.91 in Afghanistan), suggesting that more variance exists across Latin American countries than across provinces in Afghanistan.[23] The difference in happiness scores across these two contexts is surely much smaller than the difference in objective conditions.

Mean scores on the best-possible-life question were quite a bit lower in Afghanistan than in Latin America. However, not surprisingly, respondents with higher scores on that question were happier than the average. In Afghanistan, the mean score on the best-possible-life question was 4.67 on a 1- to 10-point scale, while for Latin America in 2007 it was 5.8. The mean for the world for the same year was 5.42.[24]

These findings suggest that Afghans might be naturally cheerful people or that they have adapted their expectations downward in the face of poor conditions. When asked to assess their situation in relative or framed terms, however, they are well aware that they do not have the best possible lives. Their optimism in the face of adversity may be similar to the optimism of the poor in Africa—a reflection of the need to maintain hope in the face of deep difficulties. At the same time, they are realistic in terms of how their circumstances compare with those in the rest of the world. In addition to being an example of downward adaptation, this also drives home the point that respondents answer well-being surveys differently when the frames are different.

At the individual level, Afghans seem to conform to the usual happiness patterns that hold worldwide. There is a U-shaped age curve, with the turning point being forty-eight years of age. That is on par with Latin America, but younger than the turning point for Russia and for Central Asia. With female respondents making up only 11 percent of the sample, the data are insufficient to draw any conclusions about gender. Married respondents, meanwhile, were not happier than the average. That is another domain in which Afghanistan more closely resembles Russia than the OECD countries.

One area in which respondents in Afghanistan depart from those in the rest of the world is unemployment. Unemployed people (roughly 10 percent of the sample) were no less happy than other respondents. In every other place where we have studied happiness, the unemployed were unhappier than average. That is likely a result of the blurred definition between employment and unemployment—given Afghanistan's large informal employment sector—as well as subsistence agriculture and the drug trade. It could also be that after three decades of high levels of unemployment, citizens of Afghanistan have adapted to unemployment.

The relationship between individual happiness and income is remarkably consistent across countries. Accurately measuring income in a context such as Afghanistan, however, is difficult if not impossible. There is a very large informal and underground economy, a significant part of society relies on subsistence agriculture, and there are tremendous incentives to underreport incomes. We chose to rely on two variables as proxies for income in our regressions: an index based on ownership of a number of key assets and the respondent's own assessment of his or her economic situation and prospects.[25]

Both proxy variables worked in the expected direction and correlated positively with happiness, as income typically does.[26] Some of that is likely to be driven by perceptions being auto-correlated as much as it is by real economic differences: happier people are more likely to be optimistic about the economic future as well as to place themselves higher on the economic ladder. The role of perceptions may be especially important in the Afghan context, where normal measures of economic activity and progress, such as reported income, have less significance due to the extralegal or informal nature of much economic activity.[27]

One rather surprising result was that respondents who live in Taliban-influenced areas were happier than the average. It is very important to note that these are *not* Taliban-controlled areas but those where the Taliban have a more open presence. There are some things about the south, such as more religiosity in general, that could have affected our findings, and we indeed found that respondents from these two regions reported being more devout than the average. There may also be some unobservable things about the regions where we interviewed that could strongly influence happiness but that are difficult to measure and likely have nothing to do with the Taliban.

Another instance of a contrast with most other contexts was crime and corruption. Respondents who had been a victim of either crime or corruption in the last twelve months were no less happy than the average in Afghanistan. As crime and corruption have become the norm, a significant amount of adaptation seems to have taken place, mediating their usual effects on well-being. Other variables that serve as proxies for safety and freedom from crime, such as being able to walk safely in one's neighborhood, also had no significant effects on happiness. That is a very marked departure from findings in most other places in the world, where being a crime or corruption victim is clearly negative for happiness and being able to walk safely is positive for happiness.

In contrast, respondents in the Taliban-influenced areas who reported that they had been victims of corruption were significantly less happy than the average, suggesting that there is less tolerance for and/or adaptation to corruption in those areas. Respondents in those areas also were less tolerant of tax evasion than the average (as gauged by a question that asked respondents how acceptable it was to evade taxes in their country).

CONCLUSIONS

In exploring happiness around the world, we found remarkable consistency in the socioeconomic and demographic determinants of happiness. The *modest* differences that we found across countries and regions are usually explained by *major* differences in economic contexts or in education and labor market structures. Happiness surveys not only tell us about variance in happiness across contexts but also shed light on the contextual factors. In the same vein, studies by psychologists find that most individuals have fairly stable levels of happiness or subjective well-being but that those levels are subject to short-term fluctuations.

Our look at happiness around the world supports the idea that there are different elements of well-being, some of which are behavioral and others that are determined by socioeconomic and demographic variables. The latter are much more vulnerable to day-to-day events, such as changes in employment, marital status, and income. They in turn differ across countries and tend to be more variable in the developing and transition economies than they are in developed ones. Regardless, the basic determinants of happiness across countries and across widely different levels of per capita income are remarkably similar, perhaps because of the strong role of psychological traits in determining happiness levels.

This psychological component, which is reflected in the unusually high levels of happiness in Afghanistan, also raises the conundrums posed by people's ability to adapt to a great deal of prosperity and/or adversity. Norms regarding what is acceptable vary across countries and cultures and even across socioeconomic cohorts within them. That, in turn, complicates what is for the most part a compelling and consistent story about the determinants of happiness across countries and cultures around the world. The interesting and yet complicated story of adaptation and its implications for the burgeoning "science" of happiness is the subject of the next chapter.

CHAPTER FOUR

ADAPTATION AND OTHER PUZZLES

The grumbling rich man may well be less happy than the contented peasant, but he does have a higher standard of living than the peasant.

—Amartya Sen[1]

IF THE DETERMINANTS OF WELL-BEING across peoples, countries, and cultures are as similar as the last chapter suggests, then why does Sen's grumbling rich man report being less happy than the contented peasant? How can we explain this puzzle? What does it imply about the relevance of happiness research to policy?

There are indeed very stable patterns in the determinants of individual happiness: income, age, health, stable partnerships, employment, and friendships all matter to individual happiness, in essentially the same way. The consistency in these basic determinants in turn allows us to analyze the well-being effects of other things that vary much more and that we know less about, such as the inflation rate and unemployment, commuting time, and environmental quality, among others.

This chapter draws heavily on Carol Graham, "Adapting to Prosperity and Adversity: Insights from Happiness Surveys from around the World," *World Bank Research Observer* (September-October 2010).

The role of adaptation in determining happiness around the world, however, is more complicated. While basic patterns hold when we compare individuals within countries worldwide, we find important differences in the effects of environmental or contextual factors across countries and even across some socioeconomic cohorts within them. People seem to have different norms regarding what is tolerable or intolerable in areas ranging from economic security to health, crime and corruption, and democracy and freedom. Those norms seem to mediate the effects that those particular phenomena have on well-being.

The example of Afghanistan, discussed in chapter 3, is telling. Respondents there are happier than the world average despite objective conditions that are markedly worse. At the same time, they rate their lives as lower than the world average in responding to a question that asks them to compare their lives to the best possible life that they can imagine.[2] The health arena—in which, for example, Guatemalans report being more satisfied with their health care than Chileans and Kenyans report being more satisfied than Americans—provides another example.[3] Obese people in the United States are less happy than the non-obese, but they are much less unhappy when there are more obese people around them.

There are similar patterns for unemployment: unemployment leads to unhappiness, but the unemployed are less unhappy when their local unemployment rates are higher and less stigma surrounds unemployment.[4] Similarly, crime and corruption make people less happy, but the unhappiness effects are much lower when there is a lot of crime and corruption. Freedom and democracy make people happier, but they matter more to the happiness of those who have more freedom and democracy.[5]

Adaptation is likely positive from an individual psychological perspective; it is surely a good thing that people in Afghanistan can maintain relatively high levels of happiness despite the challenges that they face. However, in thinking about the results of this in the aggregate and across a range of different domains, I posit that this same human capacity to adapt may lead to collective tolerance for bad equilibrium. In this chapter, I bring some evidence to bear on that question, with examples from the arenas of crime and corruption, macroeconomics, and health.

Another complicating as well as reinforcing piece of the puzzle is that people seem to have trouble adapting to uncertainty. Indeed, most people seem to prefer unpleasant certainty to uncertainty, even if it is associated with progress. In the economic arena, people do not seem to like the uncertainty and the shifts in rewards (and at times inequality) that accompany rapid economic growth. This is something that Eduardo Lora and I have called the "paradox of unhappy growth."[6] My research on the recent U.S. economic crisis with Soumya Chattopadhyay and Mario Picon shows that the most profound well-being effects were during the very uncertain period of the market free fall. Once markets stabilized somewhat, reported happiness recovered and even surpassed precrisis levels.

There are similar patterns in the health arena. In work measuring the well-being effects of various health conditions across individuals and countries in Latin America, Lucas Higuera, Eduardo Lora, and I found that conditions such as problems with mobility had no significant or lasting well-being effects, while those associated with uncertainty—such as anxiety, pain, and epilepsy—had significant and notable effects. Again, that suggests a preference for unpleasant certainty over uncertainty.

Understanding differences in capacity to adapt surely broadens our understanding of human well-being. Yet it also poses comparability problems. How, for example, can we compare the response of a destitute but happy peasant in India with that of a wealthy but miserable lawyer in New York? The peasant, who has a life expectancy of under sixty years and whose child is likely to die of a preventable disease, may report being very happy because of low expectations and adaptation to difficult conditions. The lawyer, who has a life expectancy of approximately eighty years and whose children are college educated, may report being miserable because of much higher expectations and adaptation to high levels of wealth. The response of either or both could also be strongly influenced by whether the individual has a cheerful or curmudgeonly disposition. Are these comparable data points? In chapter 2, I emphasized the importance of defining happiness.

Using more pointed questions that capture distinct dimensions of happiness (such as positive affect/contentment and life purpose) can help us get around this problem by clarifying which dimensions of happiness we are assessing and comparing. Still, people's capacity to adapt to a wide range of norms can make it difficult to compare their responses in a meaningful way. This chapter reviews some empirical evidence of the adaptation phenomenon and discusses the challenges that it poses to happiness economics in general and to development challenges in particular.

UNHAPPY GROWTH, FRUSTRATED ACHIEVERS, AND UNHAPPIER CRISES

We know that within societies wealthier people are, on average, happier than those who are destitute, but after that the income-happiness relationship becomes more complicated. At the macroeconomic level, the relationship between happiness and income may be affected as much by the pace and nature of income change as it is by absolute level. Both the behavioral economics and happiness literature highlight the extent to which individuals adapt very quickly to income gains and value income losses disproportionately. Rapid economic growth, particularly in developing economies, usually comes with different reward structures and increases in inequality on the one hand and volatility and increased risk on the other.

Using research on the Gallup World Poll in 122 countries around the world, Eduardo Lora and collaborators found that countries with higher levels of per capita GDP had, on average, higher levels of happiness.[7] Yet controlling for GDP levels, they found that individuals in countries with faster growth rates had lower happiness levels. When they split the sample into above and below median growth rates and above and below median income, the unhappy growth effect held only for countries that were growing at above-median rates and for those who were in the higher income group. In related joint work, Lora and I chose to call this negative correlation between economic growth and happiness the "paradox of unhappy growth."[8]

Using data from the Gallup World Poll, Angus Deaton and, in a separate study, Betsey Stevenson and Justin Wolfers also found evidence of an unhappy growth effect. Stevenson and Wolfers found insignificant effects of growth in general on well-being but strong negative effects of the first stages of growth in "miracle" growth economies, such as Ireland and South Korea during their take-off stages. The negative effect becomes insignificant in later stages.[9] Deaton found that the inclusion of region dummies (for example, markers in our equations that take into account shared traits for particular regions) makes a major difference in the results, with the significance being taken up by Africa and Russia, regions that are both fast growing and very unhappy.

Soumya Chattopadhyay and I, using Latinobarómetro data, also found hints of an unhappy growth effect, or at least of an irrelevant growth effect. In contrast to the above studies, we used individual rather than average country happiness in our equations and then controlled for the usual sociodemographic and economic variables at the individual level and clustered our standard errors at the country level.[10] When we included the current GDP growth rate in the equation, as well as the lagged growth rate from the previous year (controlling for levels), we found that the effects of growth rates—and lagged growth rates—were, for the most part, negative but insignificant.[11] In other words, we could not detect any discernible pattern between growth rates and well-being. (For a graphic summary of these findings, see figure 4-1.)

There are a number of explanations for these findings, including the insecurity that accompanies macroeconomic volatility and

FIGURE 4-1. Life Satisfaction and GDP Growth Rate, Select Countries, 1998–2008

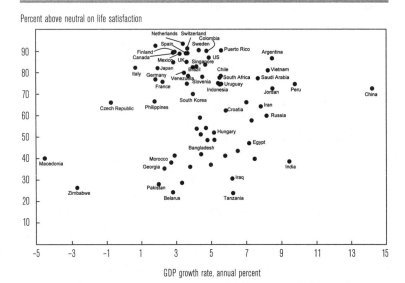

Source: Author's calculations with Soumya Chattopadhyay (March 2011) using World Values Survey (for life satisfaction) and World Bank *World Development Indicators* (for GDP growth rates).

rapidly changing reward structures and the frustration that rapidly increasing inequality tends to generate. The findings surely highlight how individuals are better able to adapt to the gains that accompany rapid growth than to the potential losses and uncertainty that also are associated with it. They also suggest that often individuals are more content in low-growth equilibrium than in a process of change that results in long-term gains but instability and unequal rewards in the short term.

Happy Peasants and Frustrated Achievers

The within-country income and happiness story is also more complicated than the averages suggest. Typically the poorest people are not the ones who are most frustrated or unhappy with their condition or the services that they have access to, for example.

Stefano Pettinato and I, using research conducted in Peru and Russia, identified a phenomenon that is now termed the "happy peasant and frustrated achiever" problem.[12] This is an apparent paradox, in which many very poor and destitute respondents report high or relatively high levels of well-being while wealthier ones with upward mobility and more opportunities report lower levels of well-being and greater frustration with their economic and other situations. That may be because poor respondents have a higher level of natural cheerfulness or because they have adapted their expectations downward. The wealthier and more upwardly mobile respondents, meanwhile, may have constantly rising expectations, or they may be naturally more curmudgeon-like (or both).[13]

The poor, some of whom rely on subsistence agriculture rather than earnings, have little to lose and have grown accustomed to constant insecurity. Recent research on job insecurity in Latin America, for example, shows that reported insecurity is actually higher among formal sector workers with more stable jobs than it is among informal sector workers. The latter have grown accustomed to employment insecurity (and/or have selected into jobs with less stability but more freedom).[14]

Other studies find an analogous urban effect in China, where urban migrants are materially better off than they were in their pre-migration stage yet report higher levels of frustration with their material situation. Their reference norms quickly shifted to reflect those of other urban residents rather than those of their previous peers in rural areas.[15]

In addition, it appears that individuals seem to adapt much more to income gains than to status gains. In a study based on data from a large panel of respondents followed over time in Germany, Rafael DiTella and Robert MacCulloch showed that most individuals adapted to a significant income gain or salary increase within a year, while status gains (such as a promotion) had a positive effect that lasted up to five years.[16] Income gains may seem especially ephemeral when one considers the frustrated achievers living in very volatile emerging markets where currencies often shift in value, where the rewards to particular skill and education sets are in flux, and where social welfare systems are uncertain.[17] And, as is discussed in chapter 1 (with the coffee mug example), individuals value losses disproportionately more than gains.

Unhappier Crises

Crises bring about both significant losses and uncertainty. Not surprisingly, they bring movements in happiness of an unusual magnitude. While national average happiness levels do not move much, they surely do so in times of crisis, although they eventually adapt back. Research on other countries suggests that the unhappiness effects of crises are due as much to the *uncertainty* that they generate as they are to the actual drops in income levels that they cause (as people have a much harder time adapting to uncertainty than to one-time shocks).

Using earlier work assessing the happiness costs of the 1998 and 2001 crises in Russia and Argentina and a daily data set from the Gallup organization, Soumya Chattopadhyay, Mario Picon, and I estimated the well-being effects of the 2009 U.S. financial crisis. National average happiness fell 11 percent, which is a very large drop for a statistic that is, for the most part, very stable across time in most countries and that certainly has been in the United States for decades.[18]

The most profound well-being effects were during the period of the market free fall—from November 2008 to March 2009, when it was unclear how deep the crisis would be or how long it would last. The drops in happiness virtually mirrored the drops in the Dow Jones industrial average (DJIA) until the markets stabilized in March 2009. At that point, reported happiness recovered and then surpassed pre-crisis levels, even though the same respondents reported their economic situation to be worse than before (see figure 4-2).[19]

FIGURE 4-2. Best Possible Life and the Dow Jones Industrial Average, 2008–09

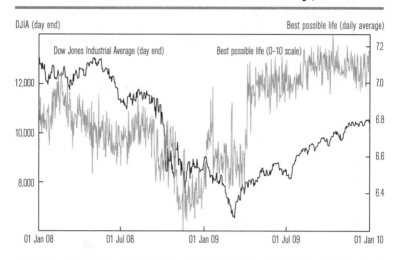

Source: Carol Graham, Soumya Chattopadhyay, and Mario Picon, "Adapting to Adversity: Happiness and the 2009 Economic Crisis in the United States," *Social Research* 77 (2010).

While figure 4-2 reports the average trends in well-being, it is important to note that there were important differences across socioeconomic cohorts. Respondents who had the most to lose (for example, people with investments in the stock market)—and therefore were the most averse to uncertainty—suffered the steepest drop in well-being and the sharpest recovery. Respondents who already were vulnerable and living in a state of uncertainty— for example, because they did not have health insurance or a job—had much lower well-being levels to begin with and were much less responsive to the events surrounding both the crisis and the recovery.

HAPPINESS EFFECTS OF FRIENDS AND FREEDOM

We have seen that rapid economic growth can cause unhappiness and that people adapt very quickly to the gains that growth brings. What about other factors, such as religion, friendships and social networks, personal liberty, participation in politics, and criminal violence? What kinds of effects do they have on happiness?

One can imagine lower average happiness levels in a relatively wealthy country that has high levels of crime. In contrast, one can also imagine happiness being higher than predicted by per capita income in a poor country that has very strong social capital. Nonetheless, it is not clear that crime rates or social capital have the same effects on well-being in every context. An important part of the story is the extent to which people adapt to both good and bad equilibriums and how adaptation mediates the effects of contextual factors on well-being.

For example, expectations may rise along with good equilibrium, such as a high level of freedom, and then the importance of freedom to happiness may increase as individuals come to expect more freedom. Expectations decline as individuals adapt to bad equilibrium (like high levels of crime); as a result, the negative externalities from bad equilibrium become less important to happiness. Downward adaptation is likely to be an important survival mechanism in times of adversity, even if it may result in collective complacency. In contrast, rising expectations and the resulting demand for higher standards may be part of the impetus for the remarkable progress that humanity has made over time in areas such as technology and health.

There is a broad literature pioneered by Robert Putnam on the importance of social capital to a host of outcomes ranging from economic development to democratic government to health.[20] Not surprisingly, there also are positive links between well-being and friendships, narrowly defined, and social capital, more broadly defined. What is harder to disentangle is whether happier people make more friends and/or interact with others more or whether friendships and social interactions make people happier.

Eduardo Lora and I and a team of colleagues at the Inter-American Development Bank evaluated the importance of friendships using data from the Gallup World Poll, which includes a question asking respondents whether they have friends or relatives that they can count on.[21] Friendships and relatives mattered more to the well-being of the average Latin American respondent than health, employment, or personal assets and only slightly less than food security (of course, it could be that happier people are more likely to have and value friendships, and Latin American respondents are, on average, happy relative to the rest of the world). The results varied according to income level, however. The rich (defined as respondents having above median income) valued work and health more than friendships, while the poor (below median income respondents) valued friendships more. Valuing religion and having access to a telephone also were positively correlated with happiness in the region. Both variables are likely to facilitate social connections and networks, among other things.[22]

Friendships most likely provide important coping mechanisms for the poor in the absence of public safety nets. Whether they serve as strong or weak ties is an open question. A well-known article, Granovetter's "The Strength of Weak Ties," showed that "weak" ties—connections beyond close knit kinships and neighborhoods—were more important to upward mobility among U.S. workers than were "strong ties" of family and friendships.[23]

It is worth noting, as I do in chapter 2, that the contrast between the rich and the poor with respect to the relative importance that they ascribe to work and health on one hand and friendships and family on the other may be a result of agency and capabilities. Work and health matter more to the rich because those assets allow them to achieve the things that they want to achieve and that achievement in part defines their happiness. Friendships and family provide the poor, who have less agency, with safety and comfort, which in turn influence how they define happiness. That brings the frustrated achiever and happy peasant dichotomy to mind and suggests that friendships and family operate more like strong ties for the poor in the region.[24] They may, of course, simply enjoy such relationships for their own sake and may have more time to do so if they are underemployed.

John Helliwell, who has done extensive research on the links between social capital, freedom, and individual well-being, found that they are indeed very strong relative to the effects of other variables that we can measure. In his most recent study, based on the Gallup World Poll, Helliwell and colleagues compared the various determinants of well-being across 120 countries in the five regions covered by the poll.[25] They found that all measures of social connections were significantly correlated with life satisfaction across the countries and regions in the sample. Respondents seem to value both the support that they get from others and the support that they give to others.

There is substantial work on the effects of political participation and the nature of government regimes on happiness. The channels through which those factors operate, however, are not completely clear. As Helliwell's work shows, the nature of a political regime matters to people's well-being, and living with freedom and good government is better than living without. Freedom seems to matter more to the happiness of those who have come to expect it than to those who have not. Veenhoven also finds that living in a context of freedom is linked to higher levels of well-being. One issue, however, is that it is difficult to disentangle freedom from other contextual factors, such as the nature of public goods and other unobservable factors.[26]

One study, by Frey and Stutzer, gets around this problem at least partially. They found that in addition to living with more freedom or in a democratic context, individuals seem to benefit from *participating* in democracy. Procedural utility is the utility that comes from participating per se, above and beyond the utility that comes from the outcome of participating. The authors used a unique data set based on variance in voting structures across Swiss cantons, in which they tested whether voters gain procedural utility from participating in direct democracy. Only nationals are allowed to vote in a referendum in Switzerland, but all may benefit from the public expenditures that result, and the welfare effects of the benefits can also be tested across cantons. Frey and Stutzer found that there was an additional positive effect on happiness that came from participating in direct democracy, an effect above and beyond that of individual traits or the variance in the level of public goods across cantons. Residents— both nationals and foreigners—who live in jurisdictions with more developed political participation rights have higher happiness levels. However, the positive effect is greater for nationals, reflecting the additional effect that comes from participating in the elections as well as benefiting from them.[27]

Work that Stefano Pettinato and I did on the developing and transition economies corroborates Frey and Stutzer's findings, although it does not solve the direction of causality problem. Using Latinobarómetro data, we found that individual respondents' attitudes about the market and about democracy were positively correlated with happiness. In other words, after we controlled for other variables such as income and age, we found that individuals with pro-market attitudes were, on average, happier than those who did not favor market policies. Not surprisingly, wealth and education levels had a positive and significant correlation with pro-market attitudes. Yet when we studied the inverse relationship, we found that happier people were more likely to be pro-market, leaving us with the usual problem of establishing causality. We had similar findings for Russia. It may well be that happier individuals are more likely to cast whatever policy environment they inhabit in a favorable light or to adapt to a range of policy environments or both.

Our findings are in keeping with those of Ronald Inglehart. In a study of nine European nations from 1973 to 1986, he found that at the aggregate country level, both political satisfaction and life satisfaction were correlated with stable democracy. The effects of life satisfaction were stronger, however, because life satisfaction trends within developed countries are fairly stable over time and seem to be correlated with other traits, such as interpersonal trust. In contrast, political satisfaction fluctuated more because it behaves like an indicator of government popularity, changing from one month to the next in response to current economic and political events.[28]

Helliwell and colleagues also tested for interregional differences in the effects on well-being of income, freedom, social connections, and corruption. The effects of social connections were lower in Asia and Africa and higher in Region 1 (the United States, Western Europe, Australia, and New Zealand) than in any other region. The negative effects of corruption were weakest in Asia and Africa and strongest in Region 1, as were the positive effects of personal freedom.

The well-being effects of corruption seem to be lower for those living in countries where corruption is a long-established feature of the status quo and people have become accustomed to it. At the same time, the value to well-being of a sense of personal freedom is higher in societies classified as individualistic rather than collectivist. Another study by Ronald Inglehart and colleagues also found that the well-being effects of freedom were greater in countries that had more of it and were more accustomed to it.[29]

ADAPTING TO BAD EQUILIBRIUM: CRIME AND CORRUPTION

Along the same vein, Soumya Chattopadhyay and I examined the extent to which individuals adapt to and become more tolerant of high levels of crime and illicit activity/corruption. Our initial assumption is simply described by the following vignette, based on my own experience.

I grew up in Lima, Peru, but lived in Washington, D.C., for many years. One day, a few years ago, I left home to go to work and tried to put my Honda Accord into forward gear. It would not move. I had been waving to my toddler twins rather than looking at the car as I walked toward it, so I got out to check whether I had a flat tire. I got quite a surprise: the tires had been stolen and my car was on blocks! I was outraged, the police were flabbergasted (tire stealing is not a common phenomenon in Northwest D.C.), and my day was ruined, in large part because I could not figure out why I had been singled out for this inconvenient incident. Had it happened in Lima, however, I would have had a very different reaction, kicking myself and saying, "Why on earth did you leave the car out on the street—you knew the tires would get stolen!" Here is an example of the same person (me) having completely different norms depending on the location.

With that experience in mind, Chattopadhyay and I used our pooled 1997–2008 Latinobarómetro data to test the extent to which the well-being effects of being a crime victim are lower in countries in Latin America where crime rates are higher (and where crime reporting rates typically are lower). As crime rates go up, citizens typically adapt, as evidenced in lower reporting rates, among other things (reporting of petty crimes is less likely to result in corrective action as overall rates go up), and less stigma is attached to being a victim.[30]

The well-being costs associated with being a victim of crime or corruption are well documented. In this exercise, we built from the fairly standard assumption that these phenomena are negative for individual welfare and queried the extent to which the costs are mediated by norms of behavior and by adaptation. In other words, are the well-being costs of being a victim of (petty) crime or of having to pay a bribe lower in contexts in which these phenomena are more common? We took advantage of the high degree of variance in levels of crime and corruption across Latin American countries to try to answer that question.

The explanation for the variance in well-being costs could be twofold. If crime and corruption are the norm, then individuals may feel less stigmatized if they are a victim of petty crime and less unethical if they have to engage in corruption to get things done. And, if crime and corruption are the norm, it is likely that individuals adapt to these phenomena because they are common occurrences. It also is possible that when crime is more common, particularly when people are in more desperate straits in general, there is more sympathy for those committing crimes.[31] Therefore, while those in countries with high levels of crime and corruption are likely to be less happy in general, there is less likelihood that they will be made unhappy by these phenomena specifically.

Our approach entailed determining the likelihood that an individual would report having been a crime victim. We did that by using the usual explanatory factors, such as his or her personal socioeconomic profile, plus the crime rate in the country that he or she lived in, plus whether or not he or she lived in a big city, and so on. We then isolated an "unexplained" probability of victimization—the victimization that we were not able to explain with the above factors—and used that probability as a proxy for differences in crime norms across respondents.[32] Our intuition was that being a crime victim would have negative effects on happiness in any event but that the effects would be lower when the unexplained victimization probability was higher.

Our results support that intuition. First of all, our first-stage regressions yielded the (expected) finding that individuals who were older, more educated, wealthier, and unemployed and who spoke the dominant language (for example, nonminorities), lived in a country with a higher crime rate, and had been victimized in the past year were more likely to be crime victims in the present year. In the second stage we found that after we controlled for everything else, being victimized in the past year had a negative effect on happiness today. However, having a higher crime norm (or an "unexplained" victimization probability) was positively correlated with happiness—for example, it acted to counter or mitigate the negative effects of victimization. It is possible, of course, that our "crime norm" variable picked up other traits that affect well-being but that we could not observe; therefore our econometric results should be interpreted cautiously. They are supported, however, by the results of other empirical studies, including our own.

Matt Hoover and I explored the same questions in Africa, using a different econometric strategy. We split the sample into respondents who reported high levels of personal security and those who reported low levels of personal security, with respondents' assessments of their living conditions as the dependent variable; we then compared the coefficients on being a crime victim. We found that the costs were *lower* for respondents who reported that they had *high* levels of insecurity than for those who had *low* levels of insecurity.

There are several plausible explanations for that finding. As in the case of Latin America, we posit that if an individual expects to be a crime victim, some of the costs already are internalized in that expectation and the actual event has smaller effects on well-being. Alternatively, victims of crime in an area where it is the norm are less likely to feel or suffer stigma effects than are victims of crime in an area where crime is rare. Or perhaps the negative effects of being a crime victim are mediated by the generally higher levels of optimism that we find among poor and more precariously situated people in Africa. All three explanations could be at play.

Chattopadhyay and I repeated our analysis of crime in Latin America with identical regressions and the Latinobarómetro data but with corruption victimization as the dependent variable. As with the crime question, the first-order question was "Were you or someone in your family a victim of corruption in the past year?"; possible answers were "yes" or "no." There also were questions about concerns about corruption in the same data set, but those were more subjective and typically linked to other optimism variables. We generated a similar corruption norm variable, based on the unobserved probability of being a corruption victim, and tested the extent to which it mediated the effects of corruption victimization on happiness.

We got virtually identical results. Being a victim of corruption in the past year was, not surprisingly, correlated with lower happiness levels. Our corruption norm variable, on the other hand, was positively correlated with happiness. As in the case of crime, being a victim of corruption appears to be mitigated in contexts where corruption is more common and individuals have adapted or become accustomed to it and there are fewer stigma effects. Also as in the case of crime, while adaptation is likely a good coping mechanism from an individual welfare perspective, it also allows societies to remain in high corruption equilibriums for prolonged periods of time.

Our findings on the effects of both crime and corruption in our Afghanistan study support the adaptation hypothesis. Neither crime nor victimization due to corruption seems to have significant effects on people's sense of well-being in Afghanistan, perhaps because people are used to so much of both.[33] Rather interestingly, there seem to be different crime and corruption norms in a few areas, which were characterized by more Taliban influence than the average. In those areas, which were happier than those in the rest of the sample, crime and corruption rates (particularly the latter) were lower and victims of corruption *were* significantly less happy than nonvictims. The findings suggest that where attitudes about the phenomena differ, individuals are less likely to adapt to the phenomena and therefore suffer greater well-being effects.

There are several ways to read these findings. Lower well-being costs are likely to make individuals more tolerant of or adaptive to such events and thus less likely to do anything about them. At the same time, departing from a high crime/corruption norm is very hard and potentially very costly at the individual level. In other words, operating honestly among the dishonest is inefficient and time consuming at best and risky or even dangerous at worst.[34] Rather than operate "irrationally" or in a costly manner, therefore, most individuals adapt to the higher crime norm. While that may be good for individual well-being and perhaps survival, it may be negative in the collective sense as it allows societies to fall into a very bad equilibrium that is capable of tolerating very corrupt and/or violent regimes. Such adaptation dynamics may help explain why regimes such as Mobutu's in Zaire or Fujimori's in Peru were able to stay in power much longer than most reasoned observers predicted.

In the same way that individuals adapt to the benefits (and also to the positive externalities) of rising overall income trends, they also adapt to the costs of rising crime and corruption trends. In the same way that income increases across time may not result in commensurate increases in well-being, increasing crime and corruption may not result in commensurate decreases in well-being as societies adapt to these phenomena.[35] There surely are tipping points in both instances, however, as crime and corruption become intolerable in some contexts.

ADAPTING TO ILLNESS:
VARIANCE IN HEALTH NORMS ACROSS COHORTS AND COUNTRIES

My research with several colleagues finds a major role for adaptation and variance in norms of health. A great deal of the variance in reported health cannot be explained by objective differences. For example, although objective health indicators are better in the Netherlands than in the United States, reports of work-related disability are higher in the former than in the latter.[36] Reports of conditions like diabetes and hypertension, meanwhile, are notoriously inaccurate, particularly in poor countries where awareness of those conditions is low. Across all countries, health norms are mediated by income and education, among other factors.[37]

Across countries, there is higher tolerance for poor health in poorer countries and less satisfaction with better health in rich ones. Within countries, while rich people are slightly more satisfied with their health than poor people, the gaps in the assessment of satisfaction are much smaller than would be predicted by gaps in quality, access, and outcomes.

Using different data sets, Lora and collaborators as well as Chattopadhyay and I found that respondents in poor countries were as likely to be satisfied with their health systems as respondents in wealthier countries. Angus Deaton found the same pattern—or lack of one—in satisfaction with health systems in the worldwide Gallup Poll. While there surely are outliers, objective health conditions—as measured by indicators such as morbidity and life expectancy—are materially better in the wealthier countries.[38] Cross-country comparisons of average levels of personal health satisfaction demonstrate a similar, although not as notable, pattern.

Across countries, health satisfaction seems to be more closely associated with cultural differences than it is with objective indicators, such as life expectancy, infant mortality, or per capita income. Average national health satisfaction is weakly and positively correlated with life expectancy, as one would expect, but it also is weakly and positively correlated with the infant mortality rate, which is counterintuitive at best!

In a related effort, Andrew Felton and I explored the effects of obesity on well-being in the United States using the National Longitudinal Survey of Youth (NLSY). We found that in cohorts in which obesity rates are high, such as blacks and Hispanics, obese people do not report being more unhappy than others, whereas in cohorts where obesity rates are low, obese people tend to be much unhappier than the mean (figure 4-3).[39] In other words, it makes one less unhappy to be obese if high levels of obesity are the norm. (These findings are on the reported well-being costs of obesity, not the objective health effects, such as propensity for diabetes, high blood pressure, heart disease, and mobility problems.)

Obesity is much more the norm among people in low-skilled professions than those in high-skilled ones. While figure 4-3 reports the results based on socioeconomic and demographic differences, in an additional exercise we looked across professional groups. We found that departing from the weight norm for one's

FIGURE 4-3. Happiness and Health: The Role of Norms[a]

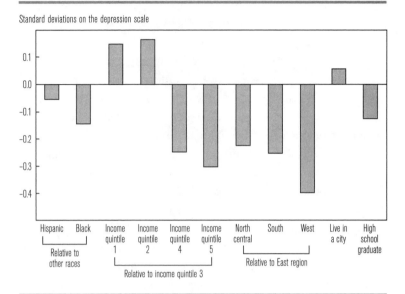

Standard deviations on the depression scale

Source: Data on file with author.

a. The base impact of obesity on happiness is 0.57: white obese people in the middle income quintile living in a nonurban area in the East who have not graduated from high school are 0.57 standard deviations higher on the depression scale than their non-obese counterparts.

professional cohort—calculated as the mean body mass index (BMI) for one's occupation, age, education, and region—had even more notable well-being effects. We also found a negative link between obesity and upward income mobility. The implications are that if a person is obese and works at Wal-Mart, he or she is less likely to move on to a better job and also has less incentive to reduce his or her weight. Thus poor health norms may contribute to creating poverty traps as well as health traps.

Another body of research is based on the Gallup World Poll for Latin America and the Euro-Quality 5 Dimension (EQ5D) index. [40] The EQ5D is a five-part questionnaire developed for the British general population and now widely used in other contexts. The descriptive dimensions are mobility, self-care, usual activities, pain/discomfort, and anxiety/depression, with the possible answers for each being: no health problems, moderate health problems, and extreme health problems.

We find that the (expected) negative effects of extreme problems in self-care and mobility on both life satisfaction and health satisfaction disappear when we include a control for personal optimism.[41] In other words, to the extent that people report negative well-being effects from having those problems, they can be explained as much by an individual's innate character traits (pessimism) as by the problems per se. The importance of inherent character traits in maintaining happiness or satisfaction is greater than the importance of (irreversible) objective conditions. In contrast, extreme health problems with pain, anxiety, and usual activities (defined as those that people expect to experience in a normal day, such as going to work, exercising, and enjoying leisure time) continued to have negative effects on health satisfaction even when the optimism control was included, suggesting that even naturally optimistic people cannot adapt to those conditions.

It is likely that people are less able to adapt to the unpredictability of certain health conditions than they are to the unpleasant certainty of others. Paraplegics, for example, typically adapt back to the level of well-being that they had before they became paraplegic, while many epileptics, who face a lifetime of uncertainty about when they will have seizures, do not adapt to that uncertainty. A number of studies of the quality of life of epileptics find that age—and in particular higher age of onset—posed significant and negative effects on health-related quality of life. Adapting to uncertainty is probably more difficult later in life, when the social, economic, and psychological dimensions of well-being are more established.[42] In contrast, older people seem better able to adapt to mobility problems and other physical conditions, perhaps because they expect to have them.

Arie Kapteyn found that people's well-being was more affected by anxiety about certain conditions, such as financial or health difficulties, than it was by the difficulties themselves.[43] Andy Eggers, Sandip Sukhtankar, and I found that innate optimism mediated the intensity of the effects of anxiety on well-being.[44] Optimism likely interacts with the anxieties related to particular conditions to determine health satisfaction. Finally, different levels of tolerance for disease and pain, which can vary significantly across countries and cultures, also appear to mediate the relationship between objective health indicators and reported health status.

All of the aforementioned findings help explain why health norms vary so much across countries, cohorts, and cultures and why quality of health care varies so much even across countries with comparable levels of GDP. Demand for better health care often is lower in societies that have poor care than it is in those that have better care and also have very different norms of health and higher aspirations based on those norms. And once again, an individual's capacity to adapt to adversity while maintaining a relatively high happiness level may be a good protective mechanism from an individual perspective, but it may result in collective tolerance for poor health systems and health status.

Finally, it is important to distinguish between adaptation across many individuals at one point in time and adaptation within the same individuals over time. Richard Easterlin, for example, points to the decrease in the United States in satisfaction with health as people age as evidence of the kinds of conditions that people do not adapt to.[45]

CONCLUSIONS

There is a great deal of evidence of the capacity of individuals to adapt to both prosperity and adversity. On the one hand, the adaptation puzzle provides us with novel insights into the determinants of human well-being, insights that are without a doubt relevant to the crafting of better public policies. Yet the puzzle also makes developing robust indicators of well-being that are comparable across countries, cultures, and socioeconomic cohorts more complicated.

Knowing that people can and do adapt and report being happy is an important policy insight. At the same time, comparisons across individuals and countries have to be taken into account. Are the responses of a happy peasant and a miserable millionaire comparable, for example, if both responses are largely influenced by adaptation and related changes in expectations? Surely the information therein is useful, but can we really compare their happiness levels if they define happiness very differently?

A question related to differences in definitions of happiness is that of whether respondents choose or select into particular definitions depending on their agency and capabilities. Does the happy peasant conceive of happiness in the Benthamite or hedonic utility/day-to-day living sense? Is the frustrated achiever trying to find happiness in the Aristotelian/purposeful life sense? The different values given by poor and rich Latin Americans to friends and family on one hand and work and health on the other are suggestive in this light.

As is noted in chapter 2, through the testing and use of many different well-being questions, we are increasingly able to distinguish between the different types of happiness and to determine whether they result in different behaviors or values and if so, how. Happiness in the Benthamite sense correlates less closely with income than does happiness in the Aristotelian sense, for example. The role of adaptation and the extent to which people choose one form of happiness over the other due to adapted expectations remains an unanswered question and perhaps one of the most challenging in future research in the field.

At the individual level, the capacity to adapt to adversity is likely a positive trait, at least from the perspective of preserving psychological welfare in adversity. Yet it may also result in collective tolerance for bad equilibrium. If entire cohorts or societies adapt to bad health and/or crime norms, it is much harder for any one individual to change or tip those norms. Why behave honestly when it is the norm to use bribes to conduct daily business activities? Why eat healthily and exercise when the norm is to eat junk food and watch TV?

The difference in norms and tolerance for adversity means that people can report being happy in conditions that are intolerable by the standards of most other people. While that information both provides a useful insight into human well-being and is relevant to policy, it also highlights the difficulties of making the promotion of happiness per se a direct objective of policy. The promises and potential pitfalls of doing so are the subject of the next and final chapter of the book.

CHAPTER FIVE

GNH VERSUS GNP?

*Too much and for too long, we seem to have
surrendered personal excellence and community values
in the mere accumulation of material things. . . . [T]he
gross national product does not allow for the health
of our children, the quality of their education, or the
joy of their play. It does not include the beauty of our
poetry or . . . the intelligence of our public debate. . . .
[I]t measures everything, in short, except that which
makes life worthwhile.*

—Robert F. Kennedy,
University of Kansas, March 18, 1968

EVEN IF THE SKEPTICS ARE correct and all of the current attention to
happiness is just a short-lived fad (which I doubt), the debate
still will have made a significant contribution by forcing us to
rethink our measures of welfare and our benchmarks of progress.
GNP is a complex, composite measure that has served the United
States and many other countries well for many years, and it will
continue to do so. No serious scholars of the economics of happiness suggest that we should toss out GNP. What the science

and the debate surrounding it suggest is that we can and should develop new metrics and markers that can complement GNP with a broader picture of well-being and quality of life.

Take the example of "High GDP Man" versus "Low GDP Man."[1] High GDP Man lives in a McMansion that uses a ton of gas and electricity; he commutes long hours to work in an SUV; he runs a tobacco company and makes $12 million a year.[2] He has no time for friends, family, or exercise. His reported happiness score is low. Regardless, all of his activities—including the production of cigarettes—are entered as positive values in our calculations of GNP.

Low GDP Man lives in a townhouse in downtown Washington, D.C., and rides his bicycle to work at a nearby think tank; he conducts research on the quality of education in inner-city public schools and earns $100,000 a year. Despite working long hours, he has time to visit with friends and to walk his daughter to school in the mornings and put her to bed in the evenings, and he runs regularly in his neighborhood park. His reported happiness score is high. Still, Low GDP Man factors into our GDP figures at a value that is 1/100 that of High GDP Man (or less), both because of the way that his productive time and outputs are valued *and* because he uses less resources, such as gasoline, heating oil, electricity, and automotive services.

For another example, compare the $397 million in oil that BP spilled into the Gulf of Mexico and the 3 million British pounds in salary and bonus that was paid to BP CEO Tony Hayward in 2009 to the $18 an hour that was paid to the 4,500 unemployed workers that BP hired to clean up Gulf Coast beaches the same year.[3] Both entered the balance sheet as positive values for GDP, but the former had an exponentially higher value than the latter. Yet the former also had disastrous effects on the quality of life and environment of hundreds of thousands of people in the Gulf Coast region, while the latter had a modest mitigating effect on that damage.

Those examples are, of course, either artifacts or extremes. Yet they illustrate the extent to which standard income-based measures of economic progress or production fail to capture important elements of quality of life. There is no "correct" metric for valuing the activities of High GDP Man and Low GDP Man, not least because normative issues are at play. Surely GDP and GNP are good measures for valuing economic activity within and across economies around the world, and much serious thinking has gone into both developing and improving them over time. Yet if one considers the way that the activities of High GDP Man and Low GDP Man affect both the quality of life of the individuals producing them and society at large, then it does not take a huge stretch of the imagination to see a role for complementary metrics and indicators.

Other metrics are, of course, available. A good example is the Human Development Index (HDI), developed by Mahbub el Huk and Amartya Sen in 1990. The HDI adds measures of life expectancy and education to more standard income data to create a broader benchmark of development progress, and it is the basis of much work at the United Nations Development Program and on global poverty more generally. Related to the HDI, "objective list accounts" of well-being are based on assumptions about basic human needs and rights, such as in Sen's capabilities approach, which highlight the needs that must be satisfied in order for human beings to be able to flourish. These objective list accounts have provided guidance on policies designed to increase literacy rates and to improve health outcomes, among other things.

The "preferences satisfaction account" is closely associated with economists' account of well-being; it is based on the simple assumption that what is best for someone is what best fulfills all of his or her desires. All else being equal, more income or GDP allows us to satisfy more of our preferences. According to this theory, more choice allows us to satisfy more of our preferences.[4]

Yet an individual's preferences do not always operate in a direction that enhances the well-being of that individual, nor are people always good predictors of what will make them happy in the future.[5] And many indicators of social and environmental stress, such as rising rates of obesity and pollution, are counted positively in GDP.

Indicators based on responses to subjective well-being questions are a distinct and complementary kind of metric. One of the primary contributions they can make is to allow us to identify and quantify differences in the welfare assessments made by objective and subjective instruments. How do we square the circle between the very different pictures that objective and subjective statistics often portray? Outcome accounts and/or accounts based on preference satisfaction would likely score High GDP Man's well-being as much better than Low GDP Man's well-being. Yet subjective well-being indicators would paint a very different picture. It is not clear that one picture is better than the other, but surely having both to look at gives us a more complete picture of the drivers of well-being in the same way that X-rays taken from different angles help a doctor to diagnosis a medical problem correctly.

The burgeoning work on happiness is surely a good start toward developing complementary metrics. Yet there is still much thinking to be done about how to translate the vast set of research metrics into measures that are operational in policy terms. One question is whether the measures and metrics should be combined in the form of a single Gross National Happiness indicator or instead used as separate indicators that capture various components of quality of life. Yet that question is less fundamental than the questions of *what* to measure and how to use the data generated.

These metrics have a great deal of potential to contribute to policy. At the same time, they could easily be misused, misinterpreted, and manipulated by politicians and pundits. Developing robust metrics that are clear and well-defined is critical. As the discussion in chapter 2 suggests, there are various definitions or dimensions of happiness, and some are more appropriate or relevant to the policy realm than others.

This chapter briefly reviews the lessons from the study of happiness that are most relevant to policy; the challenges that remain to the application of those lessons; the reasons why the definition of happiness matters; the sorts of measures that we need to develop to capture the various definitions; and the reasons why happiness is a more complex concept to measure than is income.

WHAT HAPPINESS MEASURES CAN TELL US: WHAT WE HAVE LEARNED

There is much that happiness research can contribute to our understanding of human welfare and well-being, much of it reviewed in the earlier chapters of this book. In this chapter, rather than focus on specific research findings relevant to particular policy areas, I highlight the general areas in which the research can help us design better policy.

The first area to which happiness research can contribute is the simplest. Happiness surveys allow us to value the non-income components of all sorts of phenomena, ranging from work and employment to good health and the effects of crime and corruption on well-being. Using the coefficients from happiness equations, which are based on data from interviews with hundreds of thousands of people within and across countries, we can attach relative weights to the value of a job (beyond salary), to particular health conditions, or to having been a victim of crime or corruption and compare how the costs or benefits vary across particular countries or societies.

The values are calculated in terms of marginal losses or gains in life satisfaction. Using the relative value of income to life satisfaction in the same equations, we can also calculate the values in equivalent income terms. In other words, we can calculate how much income it would take to compensate the average person for the drop in life satisfaction or happiness that would occur if the person got a divorce and how much income it would take to raise the person's happiness to the same level that it would be raised if he or she received a promotion. Similarly, we can calculate how much income it would take to account for the value of financial smoothing over the life cycle; for the impact on children's well-being of having a parent working; and for the value of belonging to a community, trusting one's neighbors, and/or being a victim of crime, among others. Of course, that value will depend to some extent on which dimension of happiness is being measured and by what question.

As a result, a policymaker considering a budget cut that could affect the availability of health insurance or the amount of disposable income, for example, would at least have a sense of the value of good health—and even of access to health insurance—relative to that of a marginal unit of income. Recent work by Danny Kahneman, for example, uses measures of negative affect ("How often did you worry yesterday?") to demonstrate how much more often those without health insurance experience negative emotions than do those with access to insurance.

A note of caution is warranted. Given that much of the explanation for variance in life satisfaction levels is unexplained and due to unobservable differences across people, figures such as those from income equivalence calculations should be interpreted as relative orders of magnitude rather than as exact dollar amounts. As such they still can provide policymakers with valuable information for making decisions at the margin.

There are other methodological approaches for making such evaluations, such as willingness-to-pay calculations and quality of life adjusted years. Yet in many instances they are ill-suited to capturing the effects of the variables at hand. Willingness-to-pay approaches, for example, are not well suited to measuring the differential costs of various illnesses or the benefits of belonging to a community or trusting one's neighbors, among other things.

Happiness surveys, while not a perfect instrument, are surely a more direct tool for doing so.

Happiness surveys also are an excellent tool for evaluating the welfare effects of institutional factors that individuals are powerless to change, including inequality, macroeconomic trends, governance arrangements, and environmental regimes. Traditional revealed preferences approaches assume that individuals are able to make a choice. Yet in many instances, individuals have no way of doing anything about such factors or even of expressing their discontent.

The effects of institutional and other variables related to the collective environment are not always those expected; they depend, to some extent, on norms and expectations. In the United States, for example, the only cohort that seems bothered by income inequality is that of left-leaning rich people! While that seems counterintuitive, the finding can be explained, at least in part, by Americans' strongly held belief that theirs is a land of exceptional opportunity (even though the cross-country data on income mobility no longer provide support for that belief).

While phenomena such as bad environmental quality and poor governance have negative effects on well-being across most people, those effects are the *least* negative precisely where those conditions most need correction because people have become accustomed to them. While that does not make the problem of "fixing" things easier and indeed may make it more difficult, it is important information for policymakers who are trying to improve bad governance or change environmental norms.

The surveys also are good tools for helping us understand behaviors that are not driven by optimal choices but instead by norms, addiction, and self-control problems. Several examples in the book highlight how happiness surveys can help us better understand both the well-being effects and the public policy implications of things like smoking, obesity, and other public health problems. Understanding the well-being effects of such behaviors and how they are mediated by norms and expectations could surely assist in the design of better public policy. Policies designed to promote healthy behaviors among the obese, for example, might well fall on deaf ears in cohorts that are caught in poverty traps because of a combination of low professional aspirations with high weight norms. For such cohorts, the incentives for improving their condition may seem very low relative to the high intertemporal sacrifices required (for example, reducing consumption today for better health over a very long time frame).

HAPPY PEASANTS AND FRUSTRATED ACHIEVERS, AGAIN

Despite having a great deal of promise, metrics based on responses to well-being surveys are not free of challenges. Chapters 2 and 4 highlight some of the problems posed by adaptation. The fact that respondents with low expectations or naturally cheerful characters may report being happy almost regardless of objective conditions creates major comparability problems, not only across countries but also across sectors and socioeconomic and other cohorts. The findings discussed above on the varying well-being costs of obesity or being a victim of crime and corruption, among other conditions or contextual factors, are a case in point.

The adaptation problem is not insurmountable. We know much more today than we did ten years ago about the many distinct components of well-being and how those dimensions can be captured by different questions. We can use these questions to better understand how the different components of well-being are affected by conditions of adversity and to what extent the effects are mediated by innate character traits and by norms and expectations. Affect levels—as gauged by smiling—are likely to vary less according to environmental conditions than are more reflective evaluations of life circumstances, such as the best-possible-life question.

Our work on Afghanistan, where respondents score higher than the world average on affect and open-ended life questions but much lower than the world average on the more framed ladder-of-life question, is a case in point. These seemingly contradictory results are actually quite informative. They tell us that people in very harsh conditions in Afghanistan are able to maintain their natural cheerfulness and perhaps even enjoy day-to-day living, which is likely a good thing given the alternative. Yet they also are realistic; they know that there are better lives to be lived elsewhere, and they assess their lives in relative terms. What we do not yet know is if the capacity to maintain personal cheerfulness and hope in the face of adversity also results in collective tolerance for bad equilibrium (a question that is the subject of my ongoing research). Yet surely these insights—which would not have come from income data alone—can inform policy. For example, they may help explain why there is such variance in the demand for public service reform across cohorts or countries and why demand often is lowest in precisely the places that improvements are most needed.

Understanding the adaptation conundrum can help us better understand human well-being or, better put, human tolerance for ill-being. We find that individuals are much more able to adapt to unpleasant certainties such as mobility problems, low levels of income, and high levels of crime and corruption than they are to uncertainty—pain and anxiety, rapid or unstable economic growth, and rapid changes in the crime rate. While some uncertainty often is necessary to achieve progress and is an inevitable result of any policy reform, information on adaptation is relevant to decisions at the margin, such as how quickly to introduce a certain reform or how much economic growth is desirable relative to other objectives.

A related question, which is critical to policy, is the extent to which some frustration and unhappiness underlies the search for progress and development. An anecdotal yet not coincidental observation is that the percentage of respondents who reported themselves to be thriving had been falling notably in the populations of both Egypt and Tunisia for the past few years, just prior to their relatively peaceful revolutions.[6]

Empirical research on migrants finds that they are less happy than nonmigrants, both residents of the areas that they immigrated to and residents of the rural areas that they left behind (another version of the happy peasants and frustrated achievers).[7] Changing reference norms also are at play. Migrants are more likely to compare their incomes with those of others in their new cities than to the income levels in the rural areas they left behind. Rural respondents, in contrast, are more likely to compare their incomes to the incomes that they themselves had the past year. Yet in the long run, it may be that the migrants derive much happiness (measured in a life evaluation rather than in a daily experience sense) from providing their children with the opportunity to lead more educated, healthy, and fulfilling lives.

Therefore, in the same way that different measures of well-being capture aspects of people's lives in adversity, they can also help us understand well-being in an intertemporal or life evaluation sense. What we do not know is what the happiness levels of the same migrants were before they migrated and a decade or more after they migrated. It could well be that there is a selection bias at play: less happy migrants choose to leave home in the first place and are unhappy in any context. In contrast, the experience of migrating may have short-term negative effects on well-being but long-run benefits, either within or across generations. (Answering these intertemporal questions is itself a challenge and requires following the same respondents over long periods of time. That is one subject of my future research).

While these findings can hardly translate into policy decisions about encouraging or discouraging migration, they can help policymakers understand the role of expectations and reference norms. Having an understanding of these factors can offer insights into the frustrations of particular socioeconomic cohorts and why, for example, the propensity for public protest is more typical in wealthier urban areas than in poor rural ones or why there seems to be a remarkable amount of public tolerance for high levels of crime and corruption in some contexts.

WHAT WE SHOULD MEASURE

At the beginning of this chapter, I posed the question of the importance of the decisions on what metrics to use—in terms of both *what* dimensions of quality of life we choose to measure and *how* we use the metrics. The answer to the latter question is likely to be different for scholars and for policymakers, with the former having much more freedom than the latter.

Richard Layard, who is deeply involved in policy discussions on well-being in the United Kingdom, makes the point that in order to use happiness research for policy purposes, we need metrics that are publicly acceptable, understandable, and measurable.[8] Heads of statistics agencies, meanwhile, worry a great deal about measures being comparable, both across individuals and countries and over time. Scholars involved in advancing the science of understanding happiness and well-being are interested in as many measures as possible, to understand both the various dimensions of well-being and the variance in how different people and countries value those dimensions.

Ideally, if scholars of well-being were in control of census bureaus and statistical agencies, all agencies would include questions in their regular surveys that capture

—life satisfaction in general terms (through happiness or life satisfaction questions)

—happiness in relative terms (through the best-possible-life question)

—feelings about life as experienced on a daily basis, through positive and negative affect questions, such as whether the respondent smiled yesterday, worried yesterday, or time spent with friends

—happiness in the Aristotelian or life purpose sense

—job satisfaction, through questions on open-ended job satisfaction on the one hand and doing meaningful work on the other

—satisfaction with health and education.

Having data on this range of questions would allow us to understand as many dimensions of well-being as possible and to see which dimensions of well-being—contentment or life purpose—the majority of people value the most and in which sectors (employment or health, for example).

While scholars can and should measure well-being in all of its dimensions, it is not clear that such a wide range of measures would make sense to a public audience or even to policymakers. Indeed, one can imagine that they could result in a fair amount of confusion.

The Office of National Statistics in the United Kingdom has just begun to incorporate well-being metrics. Its advisers in that undertaking—including Layard, cited above, and Paul Dolan, among others—have made the point that for any account of well-being to be useful for policy, it must satisfy three general conditions: it must be theoretically rigorous, policy relevant, and empirically robust.[9]

They have identified three purposes for the measures: monitoring progress, informing policy design and policy appraisal. *Monitoring* requires measuring well-being frequently to determine fluctuations over time. Monitoring subjective well-being is important to ensure that other changes that affect society—for example, macroeconomic changes—do not reduce overall well-being. *Informing* policy design requires measuring well-being in different populations that may be affected by policy, such as the mentally ill or the unemployed. *Policy appraisal* requires detailed measurement of well-being to show the costs and benefits of different allocation decisions, helping to provide a ranking of options across very different policy domains, such as employment, health, and education.

TABLE 5-1. Broad Measures of Subjective Well-Being

Measure	Monitoring progress	Informing policy designs	Policy appraisal
Evaluation measure	Life satisfaction	Life satisfaction Domain satisfactions (relationships, health; work; finances; urban/rural area; time; children)	Life satisfaction Domain satisfactions Detailed subdomain satisfactions Satisfaction with services
Experience measure	Happiness yesterday	Happiness yesterday Positive/negative affect (worried, energetic, or relaxed yesterday)	Happiness yesterday Affect associated with particular activities Intrusive thoughts related to work, home, school, and so forth
Eudaimonic measure	Purpose in life		Purpose in life Purpose and meaning from specific activities

Source: Paul Dolan, Richard Layard, and Robert Metcalfe, *Measuring Subjective Well-Being for Public Policy* (London: Office of National Statistics, February 2011).

The advisers to the UK national statistics office are planning to collect three broad types of measures of subjective well-being: evaluation measures (global assessments); experience measures (feelings over short periods of time); and eudaimonic measures (reports of purpose and meaning), as noted in table 5-1.

The breakdown of the happiness measures in the table corroborates the definitional distinctions that I make in chapter 2, where I highlight the difference between happiness as defined by daily living experiences and by life purpose evaluations. In that chapter I posit that happiness in the life purpose sense seems a more appropriate focus of policy than happiness in the daily living sense, not least as U.S. society seems more comfortable with policies that promote equality of opportunity than equality of outcomes.

Yet that does not discount the importance of understanding (and measuring) happiness in the daily living sense. The above metrics do not assign particular weights to any of the dimensions; they propose instead to collect data across the dimensions. Indeed, much of the information about daily experiences seems to be highly relevant for policy design and policy appraisal purposes. Policies that were put into place to enhance the opportunities of disadvantaged cohorts could result in making them miserable in a day-to-day sense. Well-being metrics would allow us to evaluate such effects and then reevaluate a policy before it does more harm than good.

An example from George Akerlof and Rachel Kranton's work on identity and economics is illustrative.[10] Akerlof and Kranton reference work by Robert Foot Whyte on inner-city kids in New York City gangs in which some of the brightest ones received scholarships to selective boarding schools. The scholarship kids received a much better education but did not fully fit in their new environments, and when they returned to their old environments, they no longer fit in there either. In the end, the program backfired by depriving the kids of an identity that they could relate to. The policy conclusion would be not that programs for disadvantaged kids are by definition a bad idea but that programs that take them completely out of a context that they can identify with—and therefore make them miserable in a day-to-day living sense—are unlikely to succeed.

That example highlights the difficulties of defining happiness for others and the problems that can arise in imposing a given definition of happiness. In particular, it suggests the challenges associated with imposing a purpose-based definition of happiness on those who need to acquire agency in order to achieve it. The process of achieving agency can be, in many contexts, an unhappy one. That does not mean that policy should shy away from encouraging disadvantaged individuals to acquire agency; it does, however, suggest that there may be associated well-being costs. At the least, having metrics in place to evaluate those costs provides a means to assess the trade-offs associated with a particular policy.

There are surely other examples and indeed even examples of the reverse problem. If, for example, a contentment-based definition of happiness was chosen as an objective by politicians in a particular society and imposed in the policy arena, then those individuals whose lives were purpose- and achievement-driven could end up being quite miserable!

We are far from a world in which particular kinds of happiness are being chosen by politicians as policy objectives. But these examples and the discussion above highlight an important distinction. The utility of well-being metrics and their capacity to enhance our understanding of the welfare costs and benefits of particular policies is difficult to dispute. Yet having happiness—defined in one way or another—as an objective of our public policies is a much more complicated proposition. I personally believe that the "science" is developed enough to achieve the first objective and contribute robust and comparable *metrics* to our standard measures of well-being.

TOWARD A UNIVERSAL MEASURE OF WELL-BEING

Can we achieve a universal measure of well-being that serves a function similar to that of GNP and that can also be compared within and across countries and over time? We have made great strides in the measurement arena, and we are positioned to incorporate well-being metrics into our standard measures of well-being. The British government already is doing so, and a number of the international financial agencies also are developing broader measures of well-being to inform policy. Yet that does not resolve the separate question of whether promoting happiness should be a policy objective along with promoting economic growth. In addition to the challenges highlighted above, there are still a number of issues that must be resolved in order to answer that question.

Foremost among these is the question that is the topic of chapter 2: What definition of happiness do we care about most? Do we care about contentment and experienced well-being, in a Benthamite hedonic utility sense? Or do we care about eudaimonia or life purpose, in an Aristotelian sense? Particular individuals will value one more than the other depending, in part, on what they are capable of. While scholars surely can measure both, from a societal and policy perspective, which dimension of happiness should policy aim to maximize? As noted above, some of the different dimensions may be more suitable for policy design and evaluation purposes, while others may be more appropriate as policy objectives.

At least for those in the United States, the Declaration of Independence provides some guidance. It calls for life, liberty, and the pursuit of happiness, suggesting that policy should focus on providing the *opportunity* to lead a happy life. That also is in keeping with the manner in which the majority of Americans seem to think about the choice between equalizing opportunities and equalizing outcomes. While the former objective is engrained, at least in principle if not in practice, in the structure of our laws, education systems, and labor policies, the latter is extremely controversial and finds support only among a small minority. Yet even this conclusion is a normative one that reflects *my* interpretation of American attitudes about equality of opportunity. Regardless, the issues are relevant to the measurement and understanding of well-being (well beyond the United States) and to any debate on the relevance of well-being measures to policy. As I posit in chapter 2, the absence of agency (read opportunity) suggests limitations on well-being in any context.

According to this logic, the least happy societies would be those that were founded on the *ideal* of equality but that in reality do not provide equality of opportunity—for example, agency—to all of their citizens. In other words, a society that promises agency and opportunity but fails to deliver is likely to generate more unhappiness and public frustration than one that never made the promise in the first place, even if the latter society exhibited structured injustice or inequality. In the same vein, one can imagine that a policy that aims to guarantee contentment rather than the opportunity to pursue a fulfilling life to all citizens might be unacceptable in most societies.

Yet those are extreme parameters, both in terms of assuming that the distinct dimensions of happiness are unrelated and in terms of posing the two dimensions as discrete policy objectives rather than as inputs into a broader discussion of how policies can enhance well-being more generally. Understanding all of the dimensions of happiness and developing metrics to measure them is the simple part, and doing so can certainly contribute to a more informed policy process. Selecting contentment or the opportunity to pursue a fulfilling life—or both—as policy objectives is a much more controversial proposition.

We know, for example, that having purpose in life and employment is important to happiness. But we also know that having friendships, family, and good health also matter a great deal to happiness. While different people value one or the other dimensions more, the tendency for most people with agency is to overvalue the former and to undervalue the latter. Indeed, they often do so at the expense of their own health and happiness in the long term. Any longer-term discussion of happiness as a policy objective must find a parameter within which to balance these dimensions.

There also are intertemporal issues at play. For research purposes, scholars do not need to define happiness in terms of time; indeed, they can study how it varies across time—for example, by measuring both day-to-day experienced utility and happiness as evaluated over the life course. They can measure things like pleasure and pain as distinct from life satisfaction in a broader sense and over time. That indeed works from a measurement perspective, but from a policy perspective, should we give priority to one or the other dimensions of happiness?

This intertemporal dimension also relates to the definition of happiness that is the focus of policy. Assume, for example, that we had achieved some national consensus on policies to enhance the capacity of the most citizens possible to pursue fulfilling lives. Yet helping people to acquire agency—for example, making the changes necessary to provide people with the opportunity to pursue fulfilling lives—might produce a great deal of misery in the short term. Take, for example, the above-cited case of the unhappy migrants, who are less happy once they leave their social and family ties behind and begin to compare themselves to a new reference norm in a larger, wealthier urban area.

Also relevant here is the Akerlof and Kranton story about the kids in gangs. The scholarship programs took them out of their environment in order to help them but in doing so made them miserable. That does not mean that the programs did not provide the teens with opportunities that might help them a great deal in the long term. Yet if the short-term costs to happiness are too high, then programs that are intended to provide the disadvantaged with agency or opportunity may not work in the long term.

Happiness surveys provide us with a metric to evaluate the effects of policies early on in the process. They do not, however, answer the more difficult question of whether or not the policy interventions are desirable in the first place and whether we should be more concerned about the teens' happiness in the daily experience sense or about their longer-term life prospects. The surveys can give us a better sense of what some of the trade-offs are when emphasizing one dimension over the other.

There are many other policies, such as those to trim unsustainable fiscal deficits or achieve national security objectives by fighting unpopular wars, that are designed to enhance the well-being—and indeed the life opportunities—of the next generation as much as that of current ones. Indeed, such policies often come at the expense of today's happiness, if they entail forgoing desired consumption or, even worse, sending a loved one abroad. How can or should we account for intertemporal trade-offs in happiness? Should we estimate happiness discount rates, in the same way that we estimate the value of future versus current income, for example? While that is not an unresolvable question, it is one that requires informed public discussion.

There also are issues of cardinality and ordinality. As research tools, happiness surveys are ordinal rather than cardinal in nature. In other words, there is no cardinal value attached to the particular categories, such as "very unhappy" or "somewhat happy." But from a policy perspective, should we care more about relieving misery than increasing the happiness of the already happy? There is plenty of evidence showing the deleterious effects of depression and mental illness on a host of health and other outcome variables, suggesting that there is more urgency to reducing unhappiness and misery.

Yet if we only worry about relieving misery, we will never develop strategies or policies for moving the aggregate marker forward. In other words, in the same way that economic growth policies seek to increase GNP in the aggregate, with reducing poverty as one of many objectives, presumably a policy designed to improve aggregate happiness or welfare would seek to raise the overall level of well-being, with reducing the unhappiness of the miserable as one of many related objectives.

Another question is that of whose happiness we care about most when designing policy. Politics is—whether we like it or not—likely to enter into the decision. Take, for example, a policy such as food stamps. While those of us who study poverty know that a cash transfer, which would allow the poor to make their own choices regarding how to allocate needed funds, is superior to a transfer of food to a population where national obesity rates are disproportionately high, food stamps are politically acceptable to the taxpaying and voting middle class while cash transfers are not. Thus, in the end, the policy is as much about enhancing the contentment of the middle class as it is about enhancing the eudaimonia of the poor.[11]

In sum, there is much to resolve before we can agree that developing a measure of gross national happiness is a desirable and shared public objective. Yet many countries—with Britain the clearest example—are on the cusp of developing and using well-being metrics in policy discussions. As a low-cost and risk-free first step, we could very simply consider the merits and de-merits of that approach by adding a few tried-and-true questions to our statistical collection.

Even that simple exercise could prove to be a very positive one. It would require us to re-think our benchmarks of progress and think deeply about issues such as whether we value opportunity or outcomes more and whether we value achievements or process (for example, life evaluation versus day-to-day experiences) more; we also would have to decide how much we should emphasize things like health, leisure, and friendships in relation to productivity and longer working hours.

At least for now, we can compare income across people with a broad consensus on the metric and what it seeks to measure, which is quite simply changes in the amount that each economy produces.[12] (Granted, there is lingering debate about issues such as whether the metrics underlying purchasing power parity adjustments accurately reflect a rapidly changing world economy with vast differences between the richest and poorest countries.) While we have made great strides in developing robust and comparable measures of the various and distinct dimensions of happiness, we do not yet have the same kind of consensus on the aggregate concept that we are seeking to measure and possibly aim for as a policy objective.

Happiness is, in the end, a much more complicated concept than income. Yet it is also a laudable and much more ambitious policy objective. The fact that happiness economics is seriously on the table reflects what a parameter-shifting moment it is in economics and in policy debates more generally. Indeed, at a time when so many of our public and political debates are divided and contentious, exploring new parameters and metrics that provide tools for evaluating the well-being of our citizens rather than emphasizing the roots of their divide is a welcome change.

ACKNOWLEDGMENTS

I CAN THINK OF NO better institution than Brookings to explore a new approach to assessing well-being. That is because of its tradition—unique among think tanks—of introducing innovations to policy metrics as well as to policy and because of its remarkable collection of scholars with expertise in relevant areas, from fiscal and social welfare policy to health care to domestic and international poverty, among others. It is a place that is open to new ideas and to bringing together "unusual suspects" from various disciplines to probe deeper into policy questions. And, perhaps most important, it is a place of deep collegiality, where one can discuss what may seem to be starry-eyed ideas about a topic like happiness and get the kind of feedback that turns them into viable and potentially important research questions. I value my friendships and colleagues at Brookings tremendously; indeed, they are the root of much of my happiness. I am not sure that there are many other places that would have given me the same encouragement to persist in an enterprise that at the outset was viewed so dubiously by most observers.

Specifically, there are a number of people, both within and outside Brookings, whom I would like to thank for their support throughout this venture. Strobe Talbott, since his first day as president, has been highly enthusiastic about happiness research, even when it was far removed from public attention. Charles Robinson, in whose chair I "sit" at Brookings, has become an interested follower and a generous supporter (although he may still quietly hope that some day I will do some more work on Cuba). I am deeply grateful to both of them.

Any number of colleagues have read drafts of papers, or listened to presentations, or simply asked me good questions about happiness when we met in the hallways. This list is far from exhaustive, but I would like to thank Henry Aaron, George Akerlof, Ken Arrow, Nancy Birdsall, Gary Burtless, Nicholas Christakis, Andrew Clark, Angus Deaton, Kemal Derviş, Bill Dickens, Ed Diener, Paul Dolan, Steven Durlauf, Karen Dynan, Richard Easterlin, Josh Epstein, Andy Felton, Bill Gale, Ted Gayer, Ross Hammond, John Helliwell, Martin Indyk, Danny Kahneman, Homi Karas, Charles Kenny, Marta Lagos, Carol Lancaster, Richard Layard, Eduardo Lora, Gale Muller, Andrew Oswald, Carlos Pascual, George Perry, Alice Rivlin, Belle Sawhill, Charlie Schultze, Tom Schelling, Claudia Senik, John Steinbruner, Thierry Van Bastelaer, and Peyton Young.

I cannot express enough gratitude to Soumya Chattopadhyay, who provided constant and invaluable research assistance while often managing my entire office at the same time, and who also co-authored some of the background papers. Mario Picon and Jeff Frank also provided important research support at various points. Of course, no book or project is possible without the institutional, logistical, administrative, and fund-raising support that underlies it. On this many-faceted front, I am deeply grateful to Charlotte Baldwin, Steve Bennett, Julia Cates, Gail Chalef, Yami Fuentes, Mao-Lin Shen, Kristina Server, Yinnie Tse, and Leah Wu, among many others. At the press, Bob Faherty kindly suggested the idea of a Focus book, and Chris Kelaher and Eileen Hughes were invaluable in seeing it through the publication process. Finally, on the friends and family front, I am deeply grateful to Charlotte

Baldwin, Berta Gilbert, Alec and Laurie Graham, Anita Graham and John Schenkel, Monica Graham, Merrill Hall, Rosa Miranda, Marianne Moxon, and my three wonderful children: my twins, Anna and Adrian, and my older son Alexander—to whom this book is dedicated—for either putting up with late-night arrivals from the office or for cheerfully commenting when yet another of my happiness articles showed up in their inboxes.

NOTES

CHAPTER ONE

1. Carol Graham, *Happiness around the World: The Paradox of Happy Peasants and Miserable Millionaires* (Oxford University Press, 2009).

2. See for example, Roger Cohen, "The Happynomics of Life," *International Herald Tribune*, March 14, 2011; and "China: Don't Worry, Be Happy: The Government Introduces the Country's New Mantra," *The Economist*, March 17, 2011.

3. Ben Bernanke, chairman, Federal Reserve Board, "The Economics of Happiness," commencement speech, University of South Carolina, Columbus, May 8, 2010; author's participation in a National Academy of Sciences workshop on the role of well-being measures in public policy, Washington, November 8–9, 2010.

4. See, for example, Ed Diener, "Guidelines for National Indicators of Subjective Well-Being and Ill-Being," ISQOLS white paper, 2007 (www.isqols.org). More recently, there was even a session on happiness (which the author participated in) at the World Economic Forum in Davos; see Katrin Bennhold, "Of Wealth and (Un) Happiness," *New York Times*, January 29, 2011 (http://dealbook.nytimes.com/2011/01/29/of-wealth-and-unhappiness/).

5. Sunstein and Thaler, for example, suggest that through libertarian paternalism, policymakers can *frame* consumption and other choices so that individuals are more likely to make choices that enhance their health, wealth, and happiness. See Richard H. Thaler and Cass R. Sunstein,

Nudge: Improving Decisions about Health, Wealth, and Happiness (Yale University Press, 2008).

6. Charles Kenny, "Bentham from the Crypt Once More: Politicians in Pursuit of Happiness," unpublished paper, Washington, Center for Global Development, December 2010.

7. Thaler and Sunstein, *Nudge*.

8. See for example, Daniel Kahneman and Amos Tversky, *Choices, Values, and Frames* (New York: Cambridge University Press and the Russell Sage Foundation, 2000).

9. Amartya Sen, "Rationality and Social Choice," *American Economic Review* 85 (1995), pp. 1–24.

10. Carol Graham, "Happiness and Health: Lessons and Questions for Public Policy," *Health Affairs* (January-February 2008); Carol Graham, Eduardo Lora, and Lucas Higuera, "Which Health Conditions Make You Most Unhappy?" *Health Economics* (2010); Carol Graham and Andrew Felton, "Variance in Obesity Incidence across Countries and Cohorts: Some Lessons from Happiness Surveys," Center on Social and Economic Dynamics Working Paper 42 (Brookings, September 2005); and Jonathan Gruber and Sendil Mullainathan, "Do Cigarette Taxes Make Smokers Happier?" NBER Working Paper 8872 (Cambridge, Mass.: National Bureau of Economic Research, 2002).

11. The correlation coefficient between the two—based on research on British data for 1975–92, which includes both questions, and on Latin American data for 2000–01, in which alternative phrasing was used in different years—ranges between .56 and .50. See Danny Blanchflower and A. Oswald, "Well-Being over Time in Britain and the USA," *Journal of Public Economics* 88 (2004), pp. 1359–87; and Carol Graham and Stefano Pettinato, *Happiness and Hardship: Opportunity and Insecurity in New Market Economies* (Brookings, 2002). More recently, economists have begun to use Cantril's best-possible-life question ("What is the best possible life you can imagine; how does your life compare to that life, based on a ten-step ladder?") as a gauge of happiness, not least because it has been included in the Gallup World Poll for the past few years.

12. See M. Bertrand and S. Mullainathan, "Do People Mean What They Say? Implications for Subjective Survey Data," *American Economic Review* 91 (2001), pp. 67–72; B. Frey and A. Stutzer, "What Can Economists Learn from Happiness Research?" *Journal of Economic Literature*, 40 (2002), pp. 401–35.

13. D. Kahneman, E. Diener, and N. Schwarz, *Well-Being: The Foundations of Hedonic Psychology* (New York: Russell Sage, 1999).

14. For an interesting view that disagrees with this and raises questions about making interpersonal comparisons based on this approach, see Marc Fleurbaey, Erik Schokkaert, and Koen Decancq, "What Good Is Happiness?" Working Paper (University of Paris–Descartes, October 2010). The problem with the solution posed by the authors—taking extensive biographical sketches prior to asking happiness questions—is, among others, the feasibility of incorporating it into actual large-scale surveys.

15. There also are some methodological innovations that allow us to control for individual traits, such as optimism or pessimism, in a cross-section of respondents through the use of principal components analysis of each individual's responses to a range of subjective questions. See Carol Graham and Eduardo Lora, *Paradox and Perception: Measuring Quality of Life in Latin America* (Brookings, 2009).

16. Bernard Van Praag and Ada Ferrer-i-Carbonell, *Happiness Quantified* (Oxford University Press, 2004). Microeconometric happiness equations have the standard form $Wit = \alpha + \beta xit + \varepsilon it$, where W is the reported well-being of individual i at time t and X is a vector of known variables including sociodemographic and socioeconomic characteristics. Unobserved characteristics and measurement errors are captured in the error term. Because the answers to happiness surveys are ordinal rather than cardinal, they are best analyzed through ordered logit or probit equations. These regressions typically yield lower R-squares than economists are used to, reflecting the extent to which emotions and other components of true well-being are driving the results instead of the variables that we are able to measure, such as income, education, and marital and employment status. (Cross-section work also typically yields low R-squares.) The coefficients produced from ordered probit or logistic regressions are remarkably similar to those from ordinary least squares regressions based on the same equations.

17. E. Diener and M. Seligman, "Beyond Money: Toward an Economy of Well-Being," *Psychological Science in the Public Interest 5*, no. 1 (2004), pp. 1–31.

18. Blanchflower and Oswald, "Well-Being over Time in Britain and the USA."

19. See, for example, Jan-Emmanuel DeNeve and others, "Genes, Economics, and Happiness," Institute for Empirical Research in Economics Working Paper 475 (University of Zurich, December 2010) (www.iew. uzh.ch/wp/index.en.php?action=query&id=475).

20. Jonathan Gardner and Andrew Oswald, "Does Money Buy Happiness? Some Evidence from Windfalls," unpublished paper, University of Warwick, 2001.

21. E. Diener and others, "The Relationship between Income and Subjective Well-Being: Relative or Absolute?" *Social Indicators Research* 28 (2003), pp. 195–223; C. Graham, A. Eggers, and S. Sukhtankar, "Does Happiness Pay? An Initial Exploration Based on Panel Data from Russia," *Journal of Economic Behavior and Organization* 55 (2004), p. 319–42.

22. A. Alesina, R. Di Tella, and R. MacCulloch, "Inequality and Happiness: Are Europeans and Americans Different?" *Journal of Public Economics* 88 (2004), pp. 2009–42.

23. C. Graham and A. Felton, "Inequality and Happiness: Insights from Latin America," *Journal of Economic Inequality* 4 (2006), pp. 107–122.

24. See Carol Graham and Stefano Pettinato, *Happiness and Hardship: Opportunity and Insecurity in New Market Economies* (Brookings, 2002).

25. Graham and Felton, "Inequality and Happiness"; Emily Kaiser, "The Haves, the Have-Nots, and the Dreamless Dead," *Thompson-Reuters Special Report on Inequality*, October 2010.

26. Michael Marmot, *The Status Syndrome: How Social Standing Affects Our Health and Longevity* (London: Bloomsbury Press, 2004).

27. R. Di Tella, R. MacCulloch, and A. J. Oswald, "Preferences over Inflation and Unemployment: Evidence from Surveys of Happiness," *American Economic Review* 91 (2001), p. 335–41.

28. Frey and Stutzer, "What Can Economists Learn from Happiness Research?"

29. J. Helliwell, "Well-Being and Social Capital: Does Suicide Pose a Puzzle?" unpublished manuscript, University of British Columbia, 2003; R. Layard, *Happiness: Lessons from a New Science* (New York: Penguin Press, 2005).

30. Frey and Stutzer, "What Can Economists Learn from Happiness Research?"

31. C. Graham and S. Sukhtankar, "Does Economic Crisis Reduce Support for Markets and Democracy in Latin America? Some Evidence from Surveys of Public Opinion and Well-Being," *Journal of Latin American Studies,* 36 (2004), pp. 349–77.

32. A. Oswald, "Happiness and Economic Performance," *Economic Journal* 107 (1997), pp. 1815–31; Diener and others, "The Relationship between Income and Subjective Well-Being: Relative or Absolute?"

33. R. Frank, *Luxury Fever: Money and Happiness in an Era of Excess* (Princeton University Press, 1999).

34. R. Easterlin, "Explaining Happiness," *Proceedings of the National Academy of Sciences* 100, no. 19 (2003), pp. 11176–83.

35. Kahneman, Diener, and Schwarz, *Well-Being: The Foundations of Hedonic Psychology*.

36. Rafael DiTella, John Haisken-De New, and Robert MacCulloch, "Happiness and Adaptation to Income and Status: Evidence from an Individual Panel," *Journal of Economic Behavior and Organization* 76, no. 3 (December 2010), pp. 834–52.

37. B. Stevenson and J. Wolfers, 2008. "Economic Growth and Subjective Well-Being: Reassessing the Easterlin Paradox," *BPEA*, April 2008; A. Deaton, "Income, Health, and Well-Being around the World: Evidence from the Gallup World Poll," *Journal of Economic Perspectives*, 22, no. 2 (Spring 2008); and Easterlin's response: Richard Easterlin and others, "The Happiness-Income Paradox Re-Visited," *Proceedings of the Academy of Sciences*, October 26, 2010.

38. C. Graham, S. Chattopadhyay, and M. Picon, "The Easterlin and Other Paradoxes: Why Both Sides of the Debate May Be Correct," in *International Differences in Well-Being*, edited by E. Diener, J. Helliwell, and D. Kahneman (Oxford University Press, 2010).

39. In initial research based on Latinobarometro data for Latin America, we find that respondents who report that they intend to migrate in the future are, on average, less happy, controlling for the usual socioeconomic and demographic traits.

40. Mariano Rojas, cited in Leo Bormans, *The World Book of Happiness* (Page One Publications, 2010), p. 3.

CHAPTER TWO

1. An excellent review of some of these questions, from the perspective of applying happiness surveys to policy, is Peter Henry Huang, "Happiness Studies and Legal Policy," *Annual Review of Law and Social Science* 6 (2010), pp. 405–32.

2. Jan Cornelius Ott, "Limited Experienced Happiness or Unlimited Expected Utility: What about the Differences? Review of *Happiness around the World: The Paradox of Happy Peasants and Miserable Millionaires*," *Journal of Happiness Studies*, July 13, 2010.

3. See, for example, Daniel Kahneman and Angus Deaton, "High Income Improves Evaluation of Life but Not Emotional Well-Being," *Proceedings of the National Academy of Sciences*, August 4, 2010.

4. Jon Miller, "A Distinction Regarding Happiness in Ancient Philosophy," *Social Research* 77, no. 2 (Summer-Fall 2010), pp. 595–624.

5. Ibid.

6. Ibid.

7. Ibid.

8. Rawls, quoted in Sisela Bok, *Exploring Happiness: From Aristotle to Brain Science* (Yale University Press, 2010), p. 73; and Bok, *Exploring Happiness*, p. 42.

9. Descartes's writings, cited in Bok, *Exploring Happiness*, p. 42; and Bok, *Exploring Happiness*, p. 73.

10. Anthony Kenny and Charles Kenny, *Life, Liberty, and the Pursuit of Utility*, St. Andrews Studies in Philosophy and Public Affairs (University of St. Andrews, 2006).

11. M. White and P. Dolan, "Accounting for the Richness of Daily Activities," *Psychological Science* 20 (2009), pp. 1000–08.

12. Ed Diener and others, "Wealth and Happiness across the World: Material Prosperity Predicts Life Evaluation, whereas Psychosocial Prosperity Predicts Positive Feeling," *Journal of Personality and Social Psychology* 99 (2010), pp. 52–61.

13. Kahneman and Deaton, "High Income Improves Evaluation of Life but Not Emotional Well-Being."

14. These points were both presented and discussed at a National Academy of Sciences workshop held in Washington, November 7–8, 2010.

15. Ed Diener, L. Tay, and D. Myers, "Religiosity and Subjective Well-Being across the World and the USA," unpublished paper, University of Indiana, 2010; and M. Morrison, L. Tay, and E. Diener, "Subjective Well-Being and National Satisfaction: Findings from a Worldwide Survey," unpublished paper, University of Indiana, 2010.

16. Carol Graham and Eduardo Lora, *Paradox and Perception: Measuring Quality of Life in Latin America* (Brookings, 2009).

17. Another take on this comes from recent experiments on philanthropy. Respondents who report having felt powerful recently were more likely to spend money on themselves, while respondents who report having felt powerless were more likely to spend money on others. That suggests more internally motivated behavior by those with agency and externally or socially driven behavior by those without agency. See Derek Rucker,

David Dubois, and Adam D. Galinsky, "Stingy Princes, Generous Paupers," *Journal of Consumer Research*, November 9, 2010 (http://archive.constant contact.com/fs054/1102814513565/archive/1103877214318.html).

18. Amartya Sen, *The Idea of Justice* (Harvard University Press, 2009). Ken Binmore makes similar points in his review of the book *Arguing for the Achievable* in *Science* 329 (September 10, 2010), p. 1286.

19. See Michael Ant, "Pleasure on the Brain," *Johns Hopkins Magazine* (Fall 2010).

20. Individuals with the 5-HTTLPR short alleles gene are more vulnerable to stress-induced depression than those who carry both long alleles. See Jan-Emmanuel DeNeve and others, "Genes, Economics, and Happiness," Institute for Empirical Research in Economics Working Paper 475 (University of Zurich, December 2010) (www.iew.uzh.ch/wp/index.en.php?action=query&id=475).

21. For example, the brain's response to pleasure stimuli can evolve into different addictions, in which the search for immediate satisfaction or pleasure makes the pursuit of a more philosophical or purposeful dimension of happiness mentally and physically impossible. One example is that of the Nauru Islanders, for whom an economic legacy of readily available riches, in the form of alcohol and junk food, and the lack of economic opportunities resulting from the island's dependence on phosphate exports culminated in their having the world's highest rates of diabetes and heart disease. See Ant, "Pleasure on the Brain."

22. That was done by separating the sample in quantiles of the happiness distribution and then running the regressions separately for each happiness group. See Martin Binder and Alex Coad, "From Average Joe's Happiness to Miserable Jane and Cheerful John: Using Quantile Regressions to Analyze the Full Subjective Well-Being Distribution," *Journal of Economic Behavior and Organization*, forthcoming.

23. See Carol Graham, *Happiness around the World: The Paradox of Happy Peasants and Miserable Millionaires* (Oxford University Press, 2009).

24. Our work on satisfaction with education services in Latin America, which is negatively correlated with education level, echoes these findings. See Mauricio Cardenas, Caroline Mejia, and Vincenzo di Maro, "Education and Life Satisfaction: Perception or Reality?" in *Paradox and Perception,* edited by Graham and Lora.

25. The German Socio-Economic Panel is a longitudinal, nationally representative sample of Germans that includes extensive questions on

well-being as well as data that allow for the exploration of differences in well-being across respondents from the former East and West Germany.

26. Bruce Headey, Ruud Muffels, and Gert G. Wagner, "Long-Running German Panel Shows That Personal and Economic Choices, Not Just Genes, Matter for Happiness," *Proceedings of the National Academy of Sciences* 107 (October 19, 2010), pp. 17922–26. See also Lena Groeger, "Happiness: Do We Have a Choice?" *Science Line*, January 28, 2011.

27. See Angus Deaton, "Income, Health, and Well-Being around the World: Evidence from the Gallup World Poll," *Journal of Economic Perspectives* 22, no. 2 (Spring 2008), for the Africa-U.S. comparisons and Graham and Lora, *Paradox and Perception,* for Latin America.

28. This is reported in Carol Graham, "Adapting to Prosperity and Adversity: Insights from Happiness Surveys from around the World," *World Bank Research Observer* (September-October 2010); and in Carol Graham, "Happiness and Health: Lessons—and Questions—for Policy," *Health Affairs* (January-February 2008).

29. Daniel Kahneman and Amos Tversky, *Choices, Values, and Frames* (Cambridge University Press, 2000); Richard H. Thaler and Cass R. Sunstein, *Nudge: Improving Decisions about Health, Wealth, and Happiness* (Yale University Press, 2008).

30. Amartya Sen, *On Ethics and Economics* (Oxford: Blackwell, 1987), pp. 45–46.

31. R. Biswas-Diener, Joao Vitterso, and Ed Diener, "The Danish Effect: Beginning to Explore High Well-Being in Denmark," *Social Indicators Research* 97 (2010), pp. 229–46.

32. A. Clark and A. Oswald, "Unhappiness and Unemployment," *Economic Journal* 104 (1994), pp. 648–59; A. Eggers, C. Gaddy, and C. Graham, "Well-Being and Unemployment in Russia in the 1990s: Can Society's Suffering Be Individuals' Solace?" *Journal of Socioeconomics* (January 2006); A. Stutzer and R. Lalive, "The Role of Social Work Norms in Job Searching and Subjective Well-Being," *Journal of the European Economic Association* 2 (2004), pp. 696–719.

33. David Bartram, "Economic Migration and Happiness: Comparing Immigrants' and Natives' Happiness Gains from Income," *Social Indicators Research*, August 27, 2010 (www.springerlink.com/content/j4184317421x856p).

34. Gareth Davey, Zhenghui Chen, and Anna Lau, "'Peace in a Thatched Hut—That Is Happiness': Subjective Well-Being among

Peasants in Rural China," *Journal of Happiness Studies* 10 (2009), pp. 239–52.

35. Cavit Guven, "Weather and Financial Risk Taking: Is Happiness the Channel?" Working Paper 218, German Socio-Economic Panel Study (Paris School of Economics, 2009).

36. Andrew Oswald, E. Proto, and D. Sgroi, "Happiness and Productivity," Discussion Paper 4645 (Bonn, Germany: IZA, 2009).

37. Carol Graham, Andrew Eggers, and Sandip Sukhtankar, "Does Happiness Pay? An Initial Exploration Based on Panel Data for Russia," *Journal of Economic Behavior and Organization* 55, (2004), pp. 319–52.

38. See a summary of this work in Graham, "Happiness and Health: Lessons—and Questions—for Public Policy."

39. S. Lyubomirsky, L. King, and E. Diener, "The Benefits of Frequent Positive Affect: Does Happiness Lead to Success?" *Psychological Bulletin* 131 (2005).

40. Shigehiro Oishi, Ed Diener, and Richard E. Lucas, "The Optimum Level of Well-Being: Can People Be Too Happy?" *Perspectives on Psychological Science* 2 (2007). The authors also find that the benefits of positive attitudes and cheerfulness seem higher for those at the upper end of the income scale, suggesting that cheerfulness is more useful in a benevolent attitude than in the more difficult contexts faced by the poor. In contrast, the findings in Graham, Eggers, and Sukhtankar, "Does Happiness Pay?" suggest that, at least in Russia, positive attitudes matter more to those at the lower end of the income ladder, workers who are likely to be in the service sector. The time frame as well as the contexts of the studies are quite different, as the former measures the cheerfulness of college students and then assesses their outcomes over a decade later while our study followed people already in the labor force during a five-year period.

41. David Brooks, *The Social Animal: The Hidden Sources of Love, Character, and Achievement* (New York: Random House, 2011).

42. P. Dolan, "Happiness Questions and Government Responses: A Pilot Study of What the General Public Makes of It All," *Revue d'Economie Politique*, forthcoming.

43. See Richard H. Thaler and Cass R. Sunstein, *Nudge: Improving Decisions about Health, Wealth, and Happiness* (Yale University Press, 2008).

44. Bruno Frey and Alois Stutzer, "Happiness and Public Choice," *Public Choice* 144, no. 3-4 (2010), pp. 557–73.

45. Emily Kaiser, "The Haves, the Have-Nots, and the Dreamless Dead," *Thompson-Reuters Special Report*, October 22, 2010.

46. See, among others, Martin Gilens, *Why Americans Hate Welfare: Race, Media, and the Politics of Anti-Poverty Policy* (University of Chicago Press, 1999); and Ron Haskins and Isabel Sawhill, *Creating an Opportunity Society* (Brookings, 2009).

47. Angus Deaton, "Understanding the Mechanisms of Economic Development," *Journal of Economic Perspectives* 24, no. 3 (Summer 2010).

48. See, for example, from quite different perspectives, Joshua Epstein, "Modeling Civil Violence: An Agent-Based Computational Approach," *Proceedings of the National Academy of Science* 99 (May 14, 2002); and Samuel Huntington, *Political Order in Changing Societies* (Harvard University Press, 1968).

CHAPTER THREE

1. Richard Easterlin, "Does Economic Growth Improve the Human Lot? Some Empirical Evidence," in *Nations and Households in Economic Growth* (New York: Academic Press, 1974); Danny Blanchflower and Andrew Oswald, "Well-Being over Time in Britain and the USA," *Journal of Public Economics* 88 (2004), pp. 1359–87; Ed Diener and Martin Seligman, "Beyond Money: Toward an Economy of Well-Being," *Psychological Science in the Public Interest* 5 (2004), pp. 1–31.

2. John Helliwell. "Life Satisfaction and Quality of Development," Working Paper 14507 (Cambridge, Mass.: National Bureau of Economic Research, 2008).

3. Blanchflower and Oswald, "Well-Being over Time in Britain and the USA"; Bruno Frey and Alois Stutzer, *Happiness and Economics* (Princeton University Press, 2002); Carol Graham and Stefano Pettinato, *Happiness and Hardship: Opportunity and Insecurity in New Market Economies* (Brookings, 2002).

4. Studies by psychologists, while usually based on smaller-scale samples and grounded in more in-depth questions, have tended to confirm these findings. For an excellent review, see Diener and Seligman, "Beyond Money."

5. Graham and Pettinato, *Happiness and Hardship*; Carol Graham, and Sandip Sukhtankar, "Does Economic Crisis Reduce Support for Markets and Democracy in Latin America? Some Evidence from Surveys

of Public Opinion and Well-Being," *Journal of Latin American Studies* 36 (2004), pp.

349–77; Andrew Felton and Carol Graham, "Variance in Obesity Incidence across Countries and Cohorts: A Norms-Based Approach Using Happiness Surveys," Working Paper 45, Center on Social and Economic Dynamics (Brookings, 2005).

6. The survey is produced by Latinobarómetro, a nonprofit organization based in Santiago, Chile, and directed by Marta Lagos (www. latinobarometro.org). The first survey was carried out in 1995 and covered eight countries. I have worked with the survey team for years and originally was granted access to the data; it is now publicly available. The survey is comparable to the Eurobarometer survey for European countries in design and focus; both surveys are cross-sections rather than panels. A standard set of demographic questions is asked every year. The usual problems with accurately measuring income in developing countries, where most respondents work in the informal sector and cannot record a fixed salary, are present. Many surveys rely on reported expenditures, which tend to be more accurate if less good at capturing the assets of the very wealthy. The Latinobarómetro includes neither income nor expenditures; instead it relies on the interviewer's assessment of household socioeconomic status (SES) as well as on a long list of questions about ownership of goods and assets. We compiled our wealth index from answers to questions about access to or ownership of eleven types of assets, ranging from drinking water and plumbing to computers and second homes. The correlation coefficient between the interviewer's assessment of SES and our index is .50.

7. The General Social Survey is publicly available at www.norc.org/ projects/General+Social+Survey.htm.

8. It is a nationally representative study, carried out in collaboration with the University of North Carolina and with funding from USAID, among others. More information on the survey can be found at www. cpc.unc.edu/projects/rlms/. Critics of the survey question its representativeness. Accepting that some of the criticisms may have validity, we nonetheless believe that it is an extremely valuable data set.

9. The coefficient on marriage for Latin America is positive but short of significant for the 2001 sample. For other years for which we have data, the coefficient on marriage is positive and significant.

10. Carol Graham, Lucas Higuera, and Eduardo Lora, "Which Health Conditions Make You Most Unhappy?" *Health Economics* (November 8, 2010).

11. These results are discussed in much greater detail in Carol Graham, "Some Insights on Development from the Economics of Happiness," *World Bank Research Observer* 20 (Fall 2005).

12. A study by Claudia Senik and colleagues is suggestive on this front. They find, using data from the the German Socioeconomic panel, that divorce is more likely when there are happiness gaps between couples. In other words, two happy people and two unhappy people are more likely to stay married to each other than are a very happy and a very unhappy person. See Cavit Guven, Claudia Senik, and Holger Stichnoth, "You Can't Be Happier than Your Wife: Happiness Gaps and Divorce," Paris School of Economics Working Paper 2011-01 (January 2011).

13. Indeed, the happiness-age turning point for most countries in Latin America is identical: 48.5 years. See Felton and Graham, "Variance in Obesity Incidence across Countries and Cohorts."

14. Andrew Clark and Orsolya Lelkes, "Let Us Pray: Religious Interactions in Life Satisfaction," unpublished paper, Paris School of Economics, January 2009.

15. This section is based on Jesus Rios and Johanna Godoy, "Personal Freedom, Self-Concept, and Well-Being among Residents of Havana and Santiago, Cuba," paper presented to the First Latin American Congress of Public Opinion, Colonia del Sacramento, Uruguay, April 12–14, 2007. The interviews were conducted in person, door to door, and household selection was based on standard random sampling methods based on an assessed probability that a particular household selected from a larger sample of households was representative. Interviews were conducted by university students who resided in Cuba but were trained by Gallup. Plans to follow up that study with a nationally representative sample in late 2007 were put aside after those conducting the pilot interviews were arrested and detained by the police.

16. Richard Easterlin, "Lost in Transition: Life Satisfaction on the Road to Capitalism," IZA Discussion Paper Series 3049 (March 2008).

17. This section draws heavily on Carol Graham and Matthew Hoover, "Optimism and Poverty in Africa: Adaptation or a Means to Survival?" Afrobarometer Working Paper Series 76 (November 2007) (www.afrobarometer.org).

18. The Afrobarometer is carried out with the collaboration of those survey teams and Michigan State University, the Institute for Democracy in South Africa (IDASA), and the Center for Democratic Development, among others. The survey has conducted one round each in Cape Verde,

Lesotho, Mali, Mozambique, South Africa, Kenya, Malawi, Namibia, Nigeria, Tanzania, and Uganda, with interviews of 1,200 and 2,400 individuals from each nation. The survey includes both an interviewer's assessment of the respondent's socioeconomic status and a question that asks respondents to place themselves in one of eleven income categories. The income data must be used with caution given the difficulties of accurately estimating income flows in a context characterized by seasonal variation in employment and employment of a large proportion of the population in the informal or black economy.

19. Details on the construction of our optimism variables can be found in Graham and Hoover, "Optimism and Poverty in Africa?" and in Manju Puri and David Robinson, "Optimism and Economic Choice," Working Paper 11361 (Cambridge, Mass.: National Bureau of Economic Research, May 2005).

20. One possibility, of course, is that the results are an artifact of construction: those who assessed their own status at the highest level could have, at best, a zero response even if they assessed their children at the highest level and would have a negative response if they assessed their children's level as lower than their own. In order to ensure that our results were not skewed by the responses, we re-ran the regressions based on a Tobit model where optimism is a latent variable that is reflected in the gap but truncated at 0 and 10. This specification drops all of the responses that are below zero. Most of the below-zero responses—7.6 percent of all of our observations—were from respondents in the highest income brackets who assessed their children's prospects as lower than their own; an insignificant fraction were at the lower end of the scale, poor respondents who assessed their children's prospects as as low or even lower than theirs. Yet our results were essentially unchanged with this specification. Detailed regression results are available from the authors.

21. The survey was funded by the generous financial support of the Norwegian government.

22. Distribution of samples over the provinces was according to the general population of each province. For example, 1,000 samples were drawn from the capital, Kabul City; 260 samples from the next-largest city of the north, Mazar-e-Sharif; 40 samples from Aibak, the center of Samangan province; 100 samples from Pol-e-Khomri, the center of Baghlan province; 100 samples from Kunduz City, the center of Kunduz province; 100 samples points from the city of Charikar, the center of Parwan province; 300 samples from the city of Jalalabad, the center of

Nangarhar province; and 100 samples from Jaghuri district, one of the largest districts of Ghazni province. While sampling was stratified over provinces and weighted according to the distribution of population in each province, systematic random sampling was used to draw respondents from the lists of general population provided by the Afghanistan Central Statistics Office (ACSO).

23. Author's calculations based on the Latinobarometro survey, 1997–2007.

24. Author's calculations based on the Gallup World Poll, featuring 129 countries.

25. Details are in Carol Graham and Somya Chattopadhyay, "Well-Being and Public Attitudes in Afghanistan: Some Insights from the Economics of Happiness," *World Economics* 10 (July-September 2009).

26. Respondents who received a socioeconomic assessment from the interviewers were also happier than the average, although when we include that assessment and our asset index in the same regression, the latter becomes insignificant. It is likely that the interviewers' assessments were based on asset ownership.

27. Indeed, when we include our perceived economic indicators in the same regression with the asset index, the latter becomes insignificant, suggesting that the correlation between perceived economic status and happiness is much stronger than that between objective economic indicators and happiness.

CHAPTER FOUR

1. Amartya Sen, "Poor, Relatively Speaking," *Oxford Economic Papers* 35 (1983), pp. 153–69.

2. For details, see Carol Graham and Soumya Chattopadhyay, "Well-Being and Public Attitudes in Afghanistan: Some Insights from the Economics of Happiness," *World Economics* 10 (July-September 2009).

3. See the chapter on health in Carol Graham and Eduardo Lora, *Paradox and Perception: Measuring Quality of Life in Latin America* (Brookings, 2009).

4. Andrew Clark and Andrew Oswald, "Unhappiness and Unemployment," *Economic Journal* (1994).

5. See John Helliwell and others, "International Differences in the Social Context of Well-Being," in *International Differences in Well-Being,*

edited by Ed Diener, John Helliwell, and Daniel Kahneman (Oxford University Press, 2010).

6. See Graham and Lora, *Paradox and Perception*. Gregg Easterbrook, meanwhile, has written eloquently about this in general in Gregg Easterbrook, *The Progress Paradox: How Life Gets Better While People Feel Worse* (New York: Random House, 2003).

7. There were 122 countries that had observations for both years, but by 2008, there were 129 countries in the World Poll.

8. See the chapter by Eduardo Lora and Juan Camilo Chaparro in Graham and Lora, *Paradox and Perception*. It is also possible that initially happier countries grew faster than initially unhappy countries with the same income (because they had happier, more productive workers?) and therefore that the coefficient on growth in a regression that compares the two with final income and final happiness is negative. I thank Charles Kenny for raising this point.

9. Angus Deaton, "Income, Health, and Well-Being around the World: Evidence from the Gallup World Poll," *Journal of Economic Perspectives* 22 (Spring 2008); Betsey Stevenson and Justin Wolfers, "Economic Growth and Subjective Well-Being: Reassessing the Easterlin Paradox," *BPEA* (April 2008).

10. This is to control for unobservable and/or autocorrelated errors that may apply to all individuals in one country but that are not captured by our individual-level controls.

11. It could also be, of course, that there is a lag between income growth and happiness (part of the difference between the changes and levels effects). I thank Charles Kenny for raising this point. See Carol Graham and Soumya Chattopadhyay, "Public Opinion Trends in Latin America (and the U.S.): How Strong Is Support for Markets, Democracy, and Regional Integration?" (Brookings, 2008).

12. For more detail, see Carol Graham and Stefano Pettinato, *Happiness and Hardship: Opportunity and Insecurity in New Market Economies* (Brookings, 2002).

13. Javier Herrera, for example, using panel data for Peru and Madagascar, found that people's expectations adapt upward during periods of high growth and downward during recessions and that that adaptation is reflected in their assessment of their life satisfaction. People are less likely to be satisfied with the status quo when expectations are adapting upward. Recent unpublished work on China by M. Whyte and C.

Hun, "Subjective Well-Being and Mobility Attitudes in China," Harvard University, 2006, confirms the direction of these findings.

14. Graham and Lora, *Paradox and Perception.*

15. John Knight and Ramani Gunatilaka, *"Great Expectations? The Subjective Well-Being of Rural-Urban Migrants in China,"* Discussion Paper Series 322 (April 2007); Whyte and Hun, "Subjective Well-Being and Mobility Attitudes in China."

16. Rafael di Tella, John Haskew, and Robert McCulloch, "Happiness Adaptation to Income and Status in an Individual Panel," *Journal of Economic Behavior and Organization* 76, no. 3 (December 2010), pp. 834–52.

17. A related body of research examines the effects of inequality and relative income differences on well-being and how inequality mediates the happiness-income relationship. At some level, individuals probably adapt to inequality as they do to other things and are less good at adapting to changes in inequality. I do not cover the topic here; it merits an entire paper on its own. For more detail, see Carol Graham and Andrew Felton, "Does Inequality Matter to Individual Welfare: An Exploration Based on Happiness Surveys in Latin America," *Journal of Economic Inequality* 4 (2006), pp. 107–22; and Erzo Luttmer, "Neighbors as Negatives: Relative Earnings and Well-Being," *Quarterly Journal of Economics* 120 (August 2005), pp. 963–1002.

18. For Russia and Argentina details, see Carol Graham and Soumya Chattopadhyay, "Gross National Happiness: Measuring the Impact of the U.S. Financial Crisis," *The Globalist* (November 21, 2008).

19. For a more detailed description of this research, see Carol Graham, Soumya Chattopadyay, and Mario Picon, "Adapting to Adversity: Happiness and the 2009 Economic Crisis in the United States," *Social Research* 77 (2010). For a discussion of data adjustments made necessary by a change in the question order for a subset of the Gallup respondents, please contact the authors.

20. For a comprehensive review, including of Putnam's work, see Christiaan Grootaert and Thierry van Bastelaer, *The Role of Social Capital in Development: An Empirical Assessment* (Cambridge University Press, 2002).

21. The question in the Gallup Poll is phrased as follows: "If you were in trouble, do you have friends or relatives you can count on, or not?" See *Beyond Facts: Understanding Quality of Life* (Washington: Inter-American Development Bank, 2008).

22. Andrew Clark and Orsolya Lelkes explored the issue of religion in greater detail and attempted to tease out the differences between belonging to a religion and having faith on one hand and the positive externalities that come from the related social networks on the other. They looked at 90,000 individuals across twenty-six European countries and found, not surprisingly, that belonging to a religion was positively correlated with life satisfaction. More surprising, though, they found that average religiosity in the region also had a positive impact: people were more satisfied in more religious regions, regardless of whether they themselves were religious or nonbelievers ("atheists"). The equally surprising flipside is that having a higher proportion of atheists had a negative spillover effect for the religious and for atheists alike. Their findings on religion, meanwhile, were not explained by general levels of social capital, crime, or trust. It is important to note, though, that their study took place in contexts of moderate rather than extreme religiosity and that they might have been quite different in extreme contexts, where there was more competition or even animosity among religions. See Andrew Clark and Orsolya Lelkes, "Let Us Pray: Religious Interactions in Life Satisfaction," unpublished paper, Paris School of Economics, January 2009.

23. Mark Granovetter, "The Strength of Weak Ties," *American Journal of Sociology* 78 (May 1973), pp. 1360–79.

24. In much earlier work on safety nets in developing and transition countries, I found that although safety nets—ranging from communal kitchens to group credit schemes—play an important role in protecting the poor, they also can become poverty traps because there are strong disincentives to leave the communal schemes to seek opportunities beyond them, such as those outside the neighborhood. See Carol Graham, *Safety Nets, Politics, and the Poor: Transitions to Market Economies* (Brookings, 1994).

25. They dropped roughly eight countries that did not have specifications for income. See John Helliwell, Haifang Huang, and Anthony Harris, "International Differences in the Determinants of Life Satisfaction," unpublished paper, 2008.

26. John Hudson, "Institutional Trust and Subjective Well-Being across the EU," *Kyklos* 59 (2006), pp. 43–62; Ruut Veenhovern, "Freedom and Happiness: A Comparative Study of 46 Nations in the Early 1990s," in *Culture and Subjective Well-Being*, edited by E. Diener and E. Suh (MIT Press, 2000).

27. Bruno Frey and Alois Stutzer, *Happiness and Economics* (Princeton University Press, 2002).

28. The *r*-squared for correlation between duration of democratic institutions and satisfaction is .21, while it is .85 for the link between life satisfaction and democracy. Ronald Inglehart, "The Renaissance of Political Culture," *American Political Science Review* 82 (December 1988), pp. 1203–30.

29. Ronald Inglehart and others, "Development, Freedom, and Rising Happiness: A Global Perspective (1981–2007)," *Perspectives on Psychological Science* 3 (2008).

30. Carol Graham and Soumya Chattopadhyay, "Gross National Happiness and the Economy," *The Globalist* (October 24, 2008). See also Nicholas Powdthavee, "Unhappiness and Crime: Evidence from South Africa," *Economica* 72 (2005), pp. 531–47. For an overview of the interaction between behavior and institutions and the evolution of norms, see Samuel Bowles, *Microeconomics: Behavior, Institutions, and Evolution* (Princeton University Press, 2004); Peyton Young, *Individual Strategy and Social Structure: An Evolutionary Theory of Institutions* (Princeton University Press, 1998).

31. I thank Jeff Frank for raising this point, which is the analog of the less stigma attached to crime.

32. Our basic econometric strategy was as follows. Our first-stage regression had the probability of being a crime victim (a logit equation, based on a yes-no crime victim question) as the dependent variable and a vector of controls for personal and socioeconomic characteristics (including being unemployed or not and being a minority, yes or no), along with other factors that could explain crime victimization: the reported crime rate, lagged growth, the Gini coefficient, lagged crime victimization (individual crime victimization both one and two years ago), and controls for the size of the city that respondents lived in (small, medium, or large, with the idea that there is more crime in large cities), plus the usual error term. We isolated the resulting residuals (error terms) as each individual's unexplained crime probability—for example, the probability of being victimized that was not explained by objective traits. We then included that residual as an independent variable in a second-stage regression with happiness on the left side and the usual sociodemographic controls (including minority status) plus crime victimization on the right side.

33. For details, see Carol Graham and Soumya Chattopadhyay, "Well-Being and Public Attitudes in Afghanistan: Some Insights from the

Economics of Happiness," Foreign Policy Working Paper 2 (Brookings, May 2009).

34. Francisco Thoumi has written eloquently about the costs of diverting from corrupt practices, such as by refusing to pay a bribe, when corruption is the norm. See Francisco Thoumi, "Some Implications of the Growth of the Underground Economy," *Journal of Inter-American Studies and World Affairs* 29 (1987).

35. For a discussion of how people adapt and how these strategies may vary across socioeconomic cohorts, see Rafael DiTella, Sebastian Galiani, and Ernesto Shargrodsky, "*Crime Distribution and Victim Behavior during a Crime Wave*," William Davidson Institute Working Paper 849 (November 2006).

36. Arie Kapteyn, James P. Smith, and Arthur van Soest, "Vignettes and Self-Reports of Work Disability in the United States and the Netherlands," *American Economic Review* (March 2007).

37. Thomas and Frankenburg first studied differences in self-reported and measured health based on the Indonesian Family Life Survey. See Duncan Thomas and Elizabeth Frankenburg, "The Measurement and Interpretation of Health in Social Surveys," in *Summary Measures of Population Health,* edited by Christopher Murray and others (Geneva: World Health Organization, 2000). Susan Parker and her colleagues built on that work and studied those differences using a broad-purpose, multi-topic, nationally representative survey in Mexico, first conducted in 2002 and repeated in 2005. Income predicts lower differences between measured and reported height, while the probability of having seen a doctor in the past three months increases the probability of accurately reporting weight among the obese and overweight. Of her total sample, 7 percent did not have hypertension but thought that they did and 13 percent had it but did not know it. See Susan Parker, Luis Rubalcava, and Graciela Teruel, "Health in Mexico: Perceptions, Knowledge, and Obesity" (Inter-American Development Bank Project on Understanding Quality of Life in LAC, January 2008).

38. Graham and Lora, *Paradox and Perception*; Deaton, "Income, Health, and Well-Being around the World."

39. Carol Graham, "Happiness and Health: Lessons—and Questions—for Policy," *Health Affairs* (January-February, 2008).

40. See Carol Graham, Lucas Higuera, and Eduardo Lora, "Which Health Conditions Cause the Most Unhappiness?" *Health Economics,* November 8, 2010 (http://onlinelibrary.wiley.com/doi/10.1002/hec.1682/

abstract). For detail on the EQ5D, see J. W. Shaw, J. Johnson, and S. J. Coons, "U.S. Valuation of the EQ-5D Health States: Development and Testing of the D! Valuation Model," *Medical Care* 43, no. 3 (2005), pp. 203–20.

41. Julienne Labonne and Robert Chase, "So You Want to Quit Smoking: Have You Tried a Mobile Phone?" Policy Research Working Paper Series 4657 (Washington: World Bank, June 2008).

42. See Lin Lua and other, "The Impact of Demographic Characteristics on Health-Related Quality of Life: Profile of Malaysian Epilepsy Population," *Applied Research in Quality of Life* 2 (2007).

43. Kapteyn, Smith, and van Soest, "Vignettes and Self-Reports of Work Disability in the United States and the Netherlands."

44. Carol Graham, Andrew Eggers, and Sandip Sukhtankar, "Does Happiness Pay? An Initial Exploration Based on Panel Data for Russia," *Journal of Economic Behavior and Organization* 55 (2004).

45. See Richard Easterlin, *Happiness, Growth, and the Life Cycle* (Oxford University Press, 2010).

CHAPTER FIVE

1. This example was inspired by Jon Gertner, "The Rise and Fall of the G.D.P.," *New York Times*, May 10, 2010.

2. The average salary for tobacco company executives in the United States is $14 million; the average for oil company executives is just under $4 million. See Bureau of Labor Statistics, "May 2009 National Occupational Employment and Wage Estimates: United States" (www.bls.gov/oes/current/oes_nat.htm).

3. For workers' wage, see http://money.cnn.com/2010/06/08/smallbusiness/bp_hiring_unemployed/index.htm. On BP and Hayward, see www.reuters.com/article/2010/03/05/us-bp-pay-idUSTRE6241PM20100305.

4. Paul Dolan, Matthew White, and Tessa Peasgood, "Do We Really Know What Makes Us Happy? A Review of the Economic Literature on the Factors Associated with Subjective Well-Being," *Journal of Economic Psychology* 29 (2008), pp. 94–122.

5. Ibid. Daniel Gilbert, *Stumbling on Happiness* (New York: Knopf, 2006); Daniel Kahneman and Jason Riis, "Living and Thinking about It: Two Perspectives on Life," in *The Science of Well-Being: Integrating Neurobiology, Psychology, and Social Science*, edited by Felicia Huppert, Nick Baylis, and Barry Kaverne (Oxford University Press, 2005).

6. See www.gallup.com/poll/145883/egyptians-tunisians-wellbeing-plummets-despite-gdp-gains.aspx.

7. I find this in the Latinobarómetro and Ecosocial surveys for Latin America; for China, see John Knight and Ramani Gunatilaka, "Great Expectations? The Subjective Well-Being of Rural-Urban Migrants in China," Discussion Paper Series 322, Department of Economics (Oxford University, April 2007).

8. Paul Dolan, Richard Layard, and Robert Metcalfe, *Measuring Subjective Well-Being for Public Policy* (London: Office of National Statistics, February 2011).

9. Ibid.

10. George Akerlof and Rachel Kranton, *Identity Economics: How Our Identities Shape Our Work, Wages, and Well-Being* (Princeton University Press, 2010).

11. I thank Becky Blank for raising this point in a workshop on the topic.

12. See Angus Deaton, "Price Indexes, Inequality, and the Measurement of World Poverty," American Economics Association Presidential Address, Atlanta, January 17, 2010.

INDEX

Adaptation: adaptation conundrum/puzzle, 4, 81, 83, 103–04, 113–14; certainty and, 23, 83, 114; crime and corruption and, 94–99; crises and, 88–89; economic growth and, 85–86, 89, 99; employment issues and, 87; expectations and, 90; happiness and, 41, 82, 83–84; human adaptability, 18, 22, 32; illness and, 99–103; income vs. status gains and, 87, 88; lower living standards and, 22–23; tolerance and, 82–83, 114; uncertainty and, 22, 23, 83, 88–89, 102, 114; well-being and, 112, 114. *See also* Afghanistan

Addiction, 8, 10, 39, 112, 133n21. *See also* Alcoholism; Obesity and the obese; Smoking and smokers

Affect, 113. *See also* Smiles and smiling

Afghanistan: adaptation in, 23, 49–50, 78–79, 80, 98; crime and corruption in, 78–79, 98; economy in, 78; employment and unemployment in, 77; expectations and optimism in, 77, 78, 114; gender issues in, 76; happiness in, 13, 20, 22, 30, 75–79, 80, 82, 113–14; income in, 78; realism in, 20; well-being in, 98. *See also* Taliban

Africa, 19, 73–74, 75, 77, 85, 94, 97

African Americans, 67

Afrobarometer opinion survey, 73

Age, 13, 64, 65f, 68–69, 77

Agency and opportunity: absence of, 31; acquisition of, 47, 119–20; change and, 49; definition and concepts of, 41, 51–52; education and, 40; equality of, 60–61; friends and family and, 91; happiness and, 25, 28, 31, 40–41, 43, 44, 47, 48, 60; income and, 44; lack of agency, 46; policies and, 51,